Wallsend Football Past & Present

by Dave Mooney

ACKNOWLEDGEMENTS

I would like to thank the following people who have given me assistance in putting this book together:

The staff at Newcastle City Library for their help with research of the old local newspapers records, without access to these nothing would have been possible. Newcastle United Football statistician John Allen for his help and advice. Dave Harrison for all the time he spent copying photographs for me kindly lent by many people to numerous to mention. Peter Flannery for his memories of Corinthians, Les Scullion for his recollections of Bigges Main and the late Les Todd of Northumberland FA. Also Brian Lisle, Eddie Elliott, Terry Brock and Alan Gate. Andrew Clark of Summerhill Books for his advice and guidance in having this book published.

Most of all I would like to thank my wife Pat and sons Anthony, Paul and David for their constant support and encouragement.

Dedicated to my wonderful grandchildren, Katie, Charlie and James

Previous page: Willington St Aidans, 1932 – Northern Amateur League Division Two Champions. Back row: B. Aldis (Secretary), W. Manson, R. King, J. Bell, G. Turnbull (Committee). Third row: M. Timney, R. Toman, J. Trainer, Fr R. Durman, O. Malia, T. Horne (Committee). Second row: Rev Fr T. Scriven, J. Ronan, M. Kennedy, F. Smith, Rev J. McShane. Front: M. Egan, J. Egan.

Front cover: Wallsend Boys' Clubs (Seniors), 2014-15. Back row: Ralph Starkie (Team Secretary), Jordan Robertson, Adam Tierney, Kieran Dewhurst, Michael Robertshaw, Darren Timmon, Harvey Lockwood, Martin Dowd, Kieran Tubman, Michael Starkie, Jonny Jenkinson, Steve Cuggy (Manager). Front row: Anth Brannan, Steve McCabe, (Captain), Karl Morrison, Chris Brennan, Nicky Whitelaw, Liam Stubbs, Trevor Jackson.

Publisher's note: Names have been printed from information supplied to us. Apologies if any are incorrect. We are happy to make corrections in future editions of this book so please contact us at the address or email below.

Copyright Dave Mooney 2014

First published in 2014 by

Summerhill Books
PO Box 1210, Newcastle-upon-Tyne NE99 4AH

www.summerhillbooks.co.uk

email: summerhillbooks@yahoo.co.uk

ISBN: 978-1-906721-89-3

No part of this publication may be reproduced, stored in a mechanical retrieval system, or transmitted, in any form or by any means, electronic, mechanical, photocopying, recording or otherwise, without prior permission of the author.

CONTENTS

ACKNOWLEDGEMENTS	2
INTRODUCTION	5
WALLSEND FOOTBALL PIONEERS	6
POST WAR FOOTBALL GROUNDS	10
WALLSEND'S COUNTY CUP RECORDS	12
INTERNATIONAL FOOTBALLERS	14
CUP WINNERS AND FOOTBALL LEAGUE PLAYERS	19
WALLSEND TEAMS	26
WALLSEND SCHOOLS FOOTBALL	82
YOUTH FOOTBALL	93
SUNDAY FOOTBALL	97
OVER 40S	118
LADIES FOOTBALL	120
CHARITY FOOTBALL GAMES	121
THE FIRST ELEVEN	126
INDEX	128

Wallsend Slipway 2 Heaton Stannington 1 – January 1959, Northern Amateur League. Stuart, the Heaton Stan goalkeeper, goes down to foil a Slipway attack in a game played in arctic conditions on Slipway's ground at Point Pleasant.

A LIST OF WALLSEND SATURDAY TEAMS SINCE 1945

	League	Manager/Secretary
Wallsend West End	Newcastle City Amateur	B. Lisle
St Columba's	South East Northumberland	T. Morrison
St Columba's Res	Newcastle City Amateur	T. Wylie
Wallsend Athletic	Northern Alliance	C. Marr
Wallsend Celtic	Tyneside Amateur	J. Powers
Wallsend Gordon	Tyneside Amateur	B. Todd
Wallsend Rising Sun	Northern Amateur	E. Gustard
Wallsend Rising Sun Res	Miners' Welfare	
Wallsend St Luke's	Northern Amateur	P. Middlemiss
Wallsend St Luke's Res	North Eastern Amateur	
Marine Park	Northern Alliance	T. Cassidy
NE Marine Res	Northern Amateur	
Corinthians	Northern Combination	B. Deagle
Wallsend Thermal	Newcastle & District Welfare	J. Powers
Hood Haggies	Newcastle City Amateur	F. Graham
Willington St Aidan's	South East Northumberland	J. Close
Wallsend Slipway	Northern Amateur	
Wallsend Slipway Res	Newcastle & District Welfare	
Wallsend Park Villa	Newcastle City Amateur	H. Gibson
NEERC	North Eastern Amateur	J. Anderson
NEERC Res	Newcastle & District Welfare	J. Brennan
Swans	Tyneside Amateur	J. Bace
Carville FC	Newcastle City Amateur	
Victor Products	Tyneside Amateur	K. Hutchinson
Wallsend Companions	Newcastle & District	J. Walton
Cooksons	South East Northumberland	P. Hathaway
Carville Boys' Brigade OB	Newcastle City Amateur	
Commercial Plastics	Northern Amateur	
Clelands	Northern Amateur	
Wallsend Boys' Club	Northern Alliance	V. Carrick
Wallsend British Legion	South East Northumberland	
Wallsend FC	Northern Combination	R. Cooke
Wallsend Town	Wearside	B. Bell
Lindisfarne SC	Northern Combination	A. Fletcher
Lindisfarne Athletic	Tyneside Amateur	J. Tunmore
Thor Tools FC	Newcastle & District	W. Stubbs
Orwin New Winning	Northern Alliance	N. Bains
Willington RBL	Tyneside Amateur	J. High
High Howdon SC	Tyneside Amateur	
Wallsend Miners	Wallsend & District	J. Hooks
Neptune Marine	Tyneside Amateur	
Wallsend Co-op	Newcastle Business Wednesday	S. Gilchrist
Bigges Main FC	Wallsend & District	R. Vinsome
Wallsend Town Res	Tyneside Amateur	
Neptune Athletic	Wallsend & District	
Wallsend YC	Wallsend & District	
Royal Engineers	Wallsend & District	
Wallsend Amateurs	Wallsend & District	
Sunholme Amateurs	Unknown	A. Murray
Swinburne United	North Shields YMCA	
Angus United	South East Northumberland	D. Robertson
Parsons Marine	North Eastern Industrial League	

NUMBER OF TEAMS STILL COMPETING IN 2014

Wallsend Boys' Club	Northern Alliance 1st Division
Willington Quay Saints	Northern Alliance 2nd Division
High Howdon SC	Northern Alliance 2nd Division
Lindisfarne SC	Northern Alliance 2nd Division
Lindisfarne SC Reserves	Tyneside Amateur League
Wallsend Town	Durham Alliance

INTRODUCTION

Many of you will remember Wallsend football from the early 1950s onwards with strong teams like the Rising Sun, Corinthians, Marine Park and St Luke's etc being among the best non league sides in the area. Like so many strong Wallsend teams before them, they have now gone, along with the leagues they played in – the South East Northumberland League, the Northern Amateur League, the Newcastle and District Welfare League, the Miners' Welfare League etc etc. Along with them went their league and knock out cup records and so I have had to search out old fixture handbooks and speak to ex-players and officials in order to piece together all the information before it is lost forever. Also lost are the records of the old charity cup competitions that brought out all the old rivalries and attracted big crowds – the Wallsend Charity Cup, the South East Hospitals Cup, the Newcastle Dispensary Cup, the Northumberland Aged Miners' Cup etc. I have checked with the Northumberland FA as to the whereabouts of the old trophies in order to check the winners names on the plinths but unfortunately the cups have also been lost. All the old grounds we played on, many of which have now disappeared, were not perfect by present day standards but when Saturday came around they were looked upon as the road to Wembley. Some players were lucky enough to fulfil that dream, many more went on to become professional but most just played for the sheer enjoyment of the game. Finally, I hope this history of Wallsend Football will help you to recall fond memories of the grounds, teams and games played long ago.

Wallsend Coat of Arms.

Dave Mooney
Wallsend, November 2014

Rising Sun, 1960. Back row: ?, N. Hay, ?, B. McKay, N. Dodds, H. McKenna. Front row: M. Turnbull, B. Pittam, ?, ?, ?.

WALLSEND FOOTBALL PIONEERS

In the early days, amateur football was a great attraction for both players and spectators alike. With the normal five and a half day week in the factories, coal mines and shipyards, workers didn't finish work until Saturday lunchtime and so they tended to support their local teams. Rivalry between these sides was really strong and the fixtures attracted big crowds.

Football in Wallsend at the start of the twentieth century was dominated by two clubs – Willington Athletic in the east of the town and Wallsend Park Villa in the west.

Willington Athletic's home ground was at the Clavering Field just opposite the Howdon gas works where they enjoyed great support. They were competing with all the top local teams of the time and won the Northumberland Senior Cup two years running in 1895-96 and 1896-97. They also won the Tyneside Charity Shield in 1891 beating the mighty Newcastle East End along the way. This was just a year before East End changed their name to Newcastle United.

Willington continued as a very powerful side lifting the Northern Alliance title no fewer than four times and appeared in numerous other cup finals but everything came to a halt at the outbreak of the First World War and the club had to fold. The club reformed again after the war but they were never the force they once were and although lifting the Northumberland Amateur Cup in 1939 they folded for good soon afterwards.

Willington Athletic, 1891, with Tyneside Charity Shield.

Wallsend Park Villa, whose ground was the North Road Ground where the Lindisfarne club now stands, won the Northumberland Minor Cup in the 1894-95 season and lifted the Northumberland Senior cup in 1901-02. They seemed to be going from strength to strength and changed their name to Wallsend AFC in 1912 and joined the semi-professional North Eastern League.

Although the club continued till the late 1930s, the added cost of wages and travel became too hard to sustain and they went bankrupt and had to fold in 1937. So in the space of a couple of seasons Wallsend's big two clubs had finished. I have no records of when the two clubs met in the Northern Alliance but both clubs had a big following and the rivalry must have been fierce!

The two clubs met twice in the final of the Northumberland Senior Cup; Athletic winning 3-0 in the 1895-96 final, with Park Villa coming out on top 3-0 in the 1901-02 season.

Newcastle United, 1894-95, pictured with the Tyneside Charity Shield.

REPORT FROM THE NEWCASTLE JOURNAL
NORTHUMBERLAND SENIOR CUP FINAL
22nd March 1902, St James' Park, Newcastle

WALLSEND PARK VILLA 3   WILLINGTON ATHLETIC 0
Barnfather (2), Shields

Wallsend Park Villa gained revenge for their 3-0 defeat at the hands of local rivals Willington Athletic in the 1896 Senior Cup Final with a comprehensive 3-0 victory in a game played at St James' Park, with goals from Barnfather and Shields. Many thousands attended the final and big crowds were reported to welcome back the victorious Park Villa on their return to Wallsend that evening!

WALLSEND PARK VILLA: HENDERSON, WILCOX, HICKLETON, WARD, GORDON, DOWLING, BARNFATHER, DOCHERTY, RICHARDSON, SHIELDS, J. BROWN.

WILLINGTON ATHLETIC: ROBSON, DENHAM, HOBSON, LAYERS, J. BROWN, DAVIES, CLAVERINGE, WILKINSON, RICHARSON, HARRISON, W. BROWN.

To give an idea of the quality of both teams, between 1895-1912 a total of ten players from the two clubs played in the Newcastle United first team in an era when United were League Champions three times and FA Cup finalist five times.

As the century progressed other teams came to the fore and tried to take over the mantle of being Wallsend's top side.

Howdon British Legion became the local dominant force in the 1920s winning the Northern Amateur League twice, the league knock out cup twice and the Northumberland Amateur cup no fewer than five times in seven years between 1923 and 1929. The Legion was a well-supported team whose home ground was the unattractive sounding Howdon Pit Heap but it didn't stop them attracting players of the calibre of Billy Scott who went on to play for Brentford and England, Sam Henderson who played for Chelsea and W.B. Foster who played for Newcastle United.

Right: Howdon British Legion, 1923. Back row: S. Smith, S. Henderson, J. Turnbull, N. Logan, C. Wandless, T. Brooks, J. Keivan. Front row: J. Curry, G. Curry, J. Caminada, G. Hall, J. Clark, D. Tait.

Wallsend St Luke's came to the fore in the late 1930s when they took over the tenancy of the North Road ground from Wallsend AFC. They ran two teams and attracted good support. In the 1938-39 season, a crowd of over 8,000 were reported to have packed the ground to see the first round FA Amateur Cup match against the mighty Bishop Auckland. 'Bishops' won the tie 1-0 and went on to lift the trophy beating fellow Northern League side Willington 3-0 in the final.

Left: Wallsend St Luke's 1938-39. Back row: Turnbull, Houghton, Dorsland, Linford (trainer), Bell, Maxwell. Front row: Trotter, Mann, Scott, Wilson, Rodham, Welbury.

The Rising Sun became the next big team after the war and into the 1950s. They played in the Northern Amateur League with great success before moving to the Northern Combination and then the Alliance. Although the colliery closed in 1969, the team continued competing until around 2000. Their last recorded success coming in 1990 when they finished runners-up in the Northern Alliance.

Left: Rising Sun, 1947 – Northern Amateur Champions and Northumberland Amateur Cup. Players include: Bob McKay, 3rd from left, back row. W. Lisgoe, 4th from left, back row. Dodds brothers, 1st from right, front row, 2nd from right front row. N. Richardson holding the ball. B. Daniels, 1st left, front row.

Right: Rising Sun, 1950, Northumberland Amateur Cup, Heddon Homes Cup, Northern Amateur Cup. Players, back row: J. Grieves, R. McKay, W. Lisgo, W. Rigby, W. Dobbs. Front row: B. Daniels, A. Muir, D. Redhead, Mascot B. Richardson, N. Richardson, R. Heron, Walter Dodds. Far right: E. Gustard who managed the team for many years.

Corinthians also had a very strong side in the 1950s; winning the South East Northumberland League title five times in as many years along with numerous other trophies. They also ran a very successful junior team. Corinthians home ground was at Heaton Terrace, North Shields, before moving back to Wallsend where they played at Bigges Main.

Left: Corinthians, 1955-56. Back row: R. Chambers, D. Johnstone, P. Moore, H. Appleby, ?, ?, B. Beautiman. Front row: B. Higgins, ?, B. Walker, S. Jackson, H. Laverick, K. Flannery, ?

Wallsend Athletic had a very strong side in the 1960s. Managed by Cyril Marr and Bob Canfield, they won the Tyneside Amateur League three times and the League Cup twice before moving to the Northern Alliance.

Right: Wallsend Athletic, 1960. Back row: B. Canfield, J. McGhee, J. Tunmore, T. Timney, ?, ?, C. Marr. Front row: R. Rooney, ?, Conroy, J. McDonald, ?, ?.

Wallsend Gordon ran by Billy Todd always had strong sides and won the Tyneside Amateur League in 1967-68.

Wallsend Celtic managed by Joe Powers and Joe Justice were a very good team in the late 1960s and early '70s and were the Tyneside Amateur League Champions in the 1972-73 season.

Marine Park set the pace as Wallsend's top team in the 1970s; winning the Northern Alliance twice 1972-73 and 1973-74 and also winning the League Cup on four occasions 1972-73, 1973-74, 1974-75, 1976-77. They also lifted the Northumberland Minor Cup in the 1966-67 season.

Above: Wallsend Gordon FC, 1966. Back row: Milne, Oliver, Taylor, Allen, Dewhurst, Hastings. Front row: Clarke, Playle, Warne, Keenan, Dowling.

Right: Marine Park FC, 1975 – Northern Alliance League. Back row: T. Cassidy (Co-manager), T. Young, R. Lodge (Co-manager), A. Smith, Clark, A. Adams, R. Macklin, Gallagher, C. Fotland. Front row: J. Hamilton, R. Stabler, G. Stoneman, R. Percy, M. Barry, Mascot Gordon Ogle.

Wallsend Town under manager John Watson lifted the Wearside League title in the 1978-79 season. Based at the Sports Centre, they looked to be going on to greater things, but after moving to the Alliance and changing grounds more than once they folded.

Wallsend Town reformed under a totally different management in the 1990s. In the 2014-15 season, Wallsend Town are playing in the Durham Alliance.

POST WAR FOOTBALL GROUNDS

St Peter's Road with five pitches in full use every week of the season, it was the main focal point of Wallsend football, still in use.

Marine Park had two lovely pitches and a clubhouse on this enclosed ground, it's now built on.

Hood Haggies had their own enclosed ground behind the Albion Pub area of Howdon, now built on.

Slipway Sports Ground a well-cared for enclosed ground adjacent to Marine Parks, now built on.

NEERC, lovely enclosed ground at the top of Kings Road South, now the Covers housing estate.

NEEB Sports Pavillion, Kings Road South, Wallsend in the 1970s.

Rising Sun always a well looked after ground with two pitches, is still in use and is home to a number of Saturday and Sunday teams.

Thermal enclosed ground at Bigges Main on what is now part of the golf course.

Sports Centre, with two pitches, was home to Wallsend FC for quite a few seasons. Although the ground is still there, it is on the golf club site and is not used.

Powder Monkey, next to the railway lines was used by Bigges Main and the Coronation Club in the 1940s and '50s.

Parsons at the top of Station Road, where the bowling alley now stands, had a lovely enclosed ground with two beautiful pitches.

Naval Yard, like Parsons not a Wallsend club, but they had their ground on what is now part of the Wallsend Golf Course next to the railway lines. You can still see the wrought iron gates with the Vickers Armstrong emblem on them.

Wallsend Schools, 1964. A crowd over 3,000 saw Wallsend under 15s go down 1-3 to Blackburn in the English School Trophy, 3rd round at the Rising Sun Ground.

Swans Recreation Ground (The Rec). Always considered a Wallsend Ground, it was home to Swans, Park Villa, Wallsend Athletic and various Wallsend teams down the years.

Langdale Centre just off Mitford Gardens, Howdon; an enclosed ground currently the home of Wallsend Town.

Wallsend Boys' Club – a magnificent new enclosed ground at Rheyt Avenue on what was part of the golf course. It contains four full size pitches and several small sided pitches and the Boys' Club now run a senior team and junior sides ranging from under sevens to under eighteens.

North Road Ground, which once had a reported crowd of 8,000 for a match, was the biggest ground in Wallsend. It had two turnstiles on Douglas Street at the main entrance, two on West Street and two down the alley at the far side of the ground. Home to a number of prominent clubs down the years, it was sold in the early 1960s and the Lindisfarne Club was built on the site. The terracing behind both goals was removed and a new pitch was laid but the ground was finally sold for building in the 1990s.

Hospital Field, at the back of the Hadrian Fever Hospital beside Wallsend Burn, had two pitches and was home to many of the early Wallsend pioneering football teams. Although the field is still there, it hasn't been used since the 1950s.

Western Field although a school field, was used by various youth and senior teams.

Wallsend Charity Cup Final, 1956. A big crowd turns out at North Road to watch Heaton Stannington beat Corinthians 2-0.

The following newspaper report of a Charity Cup Final at the North Road Ground in the 1950s describes an entertaining game played before a crowd of almost 3,000:

WALLEND CHARITY CUP FINAL, MARCH 1957
RISING SUN 4 SWANS 3

The 1957 final of the Wallsend Charity Cup was played at North Road Ground and attracted a crowd of almost 3,000 and was reported to be one of the most exiting finals ever with the Rising Sun winning by the odd goal in seven. The Sun took an early lead through Brown before Swans hit back twice, scoring through Laskey and Nichol to give them a 2-1 interval lead. The second half continued to be as entertaining as the first before the Sun levelled through Miller only for Swans to take the lead again through Kiddie. Swans were reduced to ten men on 75 minutes when Haycock was injured and had to leave the field and although they battled bravely the sun began to make the extra man count and Lindsay equalised in the 86th minute to take the game into extra time. Swans ten men gave as good as they got in the extra period nearly snatching the lead on a couple of occasions but were beaten in the 120th minute when Brown smashed in his second goal of the game for the Sun's winner.

Rising Sun: Wilson, Adams, Lindsay, Hay, McKay, Will Dodds, Wal Dodds, Miller, Brown, Brownlee, Knox.

Swans: Haywood, Watson, Allison, Rennison, Haycock, McKenzie, Laskie, Kiddie, Hayes, Conway, Nichol.

WALLSEND'S COUNTY CUP RECORDS

NORTHUMBERLAND SENIOR CUP

Willington Athletic Winners 1895-96 and 1896-97
Wallsend Park Villa Winners 1901-02

NORTHUMBERLAND AMATEUR CUP

Howdon British Legion	Winners 1922-23, 1924-25, 1925-26, 1926-27, 1928-29
Bigges Main	Winners 1933-34
Swans	Winners 1934-35
Wallsend Gordon	Winners 1937-38
Willington Athletic	Winners 1938-39
Wallsend Rising Sun	Winners 1946-47, 1949-50, 1954-55
Wallsend FC	Winners 1968-69

Left: Wallsend Gordon in the 1920s. Back row: J. Smith, S. Thompson, ?, J. Lemon, J. Francis, T. Strakers, T. Booth, B. Swan, J. Ward, A. Senior, T. Davidson. Front row: H. McMurray, A. Marshall, C. Dirlands, J. Aitcheson, G. Fawcett, M. Malin, J. Stephenson.

NORTHUMBELAND MINOR CUP

Wallsend Park Villa	Winners 1895	Wallsend Elm Villa	Winners 1911
Wallsend Celtic	Winners 1933	Swans	Winners 1935
Wallsend St Luke's	Winners 1940	Marine Park	Winners 1967
Wallsend Rising Sun	Winners 1973	Orwin New Winning	Winners 1994

NORTHUMBERLAND CHALLENGE BOWL

Willington Athletic	Winners 1890-01, 1891-92, 1895-96
Wallsend Park Villa / Wallsend AFC	Winners 1903-04, 1906-07, 1929-30

NORTHUMBERLAND BENEVOLENT BOWL
(replaced Amateur Cup)

Wallsend Town   Winners 2006-07

NORTHUMBERLAND FA MIDWEEK CHALLENGE CUP

Willington Wednesday   Winners 1911-12
Wallsend Tradesmen   Winners 1930-31, 1931-32, 1933-34

NORTHUMBERLAND SUNDAY COUNTY KNOCK OUT CUP

Wallsend Labour Club   Winners 1991-92, 1992-93, 1994-95

NORTHUMBERLAND JUNIOR CUP (under 18)

Bewick Athletic	Winners 1896-97
Rosehill Villa	Winners 1909-10
Wallsend Rising Sun	Winners 1952-53, 1970-71, 1976-77
Corinthians	Winners 1960-61, 1962-63
Wallsend Boys' Club	Winners 1980-81, 1981-82

Top right: Bewick Athletic Jnrs, 1898 – Northumberland Jnr Cup Winners the previous year.

Below right: Wallsend Corinthians Jnr, 1959. Back row: ?, D. Winskill, S. Craig, J. McNally, Stephenson, M. Cuskern, G. Parkin, G. Little, D. Burns. Front row: J. McCrae, P. Flaherty, D. Lackenby, L. Cox, M. Dunne.

Below: Wallsend Rising Sun Jnrs, 1971. Back row: P. Kirkley, J. Tubman, K. Dodds, G. Sutherland, L. Wynn, J. Graham, E. Steele, A. Waddle, I. Kirkpatrick, B. Storey, T. Clarke, G. Gilchrist, W. Phillips. Front row: H. Watson, D. Dugdale, M. Taylor, M. Joyce, B. Sloan, S. O'Donnell

INTERNATIONAL FOOTBALLERS

A number of Wallsend players, by that I mean either born in the town or played for one of its teams, have gone on to represent their country.

Henry 'Sharkey' Chambers – Rosehill Villa
Henry, an England schoolboy international born in Willington Quay on 17th November 1896, signed for Liverpool from North Shields Athletic in April 1915. Because of the First World War he didn't make his debut till 1919. He went on to make 339 appearances for the Merseysiders scoring 151 times! Collecting two championship winners medals along the way. He made his international debut against Wales in 1921 and went on to win eight caps for this country. He moved to West Bromich Albion in 1928 playing 46 times and scoring five goals before retiring in 1929.

Billy Scott – Willington Athletic
Born in Willington Quay on 6th December 1907, a clever inside forward, Billy played for Willington Athletic before signing for Brentford where he won one England cap in 1936. Billy finished his pro career at Middlesbrough.

Sharkey Chambers – Liverpool and England.

Frank Cuggy – Bigges Main Celtic, Willington Athletic
Born in Walker on 16th June 1889, Frank joined Sunderland from Willington Athletic in 1909 and made his first team debut in February 1913. Sunderland went on to become League Champions that season and just missed out on the double when they lost the FA Cup Final to Aston Villa 0-1.

In his twelve years at Roker, he made a total of 190 appearances and scored 4 goals. Frank won two England caps in 1913 and 1914 both against Northern Ireland before the outbreak of the war interrupted his career.

After the war he returned to Sunderland for the 1919-20 season but finally left the club in May 1921 to become manager of Wallsend AFC. He spent two years as manager of Wallsend who played in the semi-pro North Eastern League before accepting a five year contract to manage Celta Vigo in the Spanish League.

Frank Cuggy – Sunderland AFC and England.

Billy Scott – Brentford and England.

Albert Stubbins – Bigges Main Celtic
Born in Wallsend, Albert signed for Newcastle United in 1936 and made his debut against Swansea Town on 3rd April 1938. Albert was a remarkable striker hitting an amazing 231 goals in five wartime seasons – five times hitting 40 or more goals in a season. Capped by England during the war and in victory internationals, Albert stunned the Newcastle supporters when he moved to Liverpool in September 1946 for a then massive £12,500 fee. He helped the Reds to lift the title in 1947 and to the FA Cup Final in 1950. He hit 83 goals for Liverpool before retiring in 1954.

Albert Stubbins – Former Newcastle United and Liverpool centre forward.

Michael Carrick – Wallsend Boys' Club

Born in Wallsend on 28th July 1981, Michael signed for West Ham United from Wallsend Boys' Club in 1997 and made his senior debut in 1998. He went on to make 136 appearances for the Hammers before moving to Spurs for £3.5 million in 2004. He was then transferred to Manchester United for £18 million in 2006 where he continues to carve out a great career. Michael has been capped 24 times for England, has five Premier League Winners medals, one Champions League Winners medal and a FIFA World Club Cup title.

Alan Thompson – Wallsend Boys' Club

Born in Wallsend on 22nd December 1973, Alan joined Newcastle United from Wallsend Boys' Club in 1989. He made his debut for the Magpies in 1991 and went on to make 13 appearances before moving to Bolton Wanderers in 1993 where he made 157 appearances. He signed for Aston Villa in 1998 and then onto Celtic in 2000 where he won his only England cap against Sweden in 2004. Alan was then transferred to Leeds United in 2007 and then turned out briefly for Hartlepool United before calling an end to his playing career.

Honours: one England Cap. Newcastle United – Division One title. Bolton Wanderers – Division One title. Celtic – Scottish Premier League, four titles. Scottish FA Cup Winner, three times. Scottish League Cup Winner twice

Michael Carrick in England colours.

Jock Rutherford – Willington Athletic

Although born across the border in Percy Main, Jock played for Willington Athletic before signing for Newcastle United in 1902. He amassed a total of 336 appearances for the Magpies scoring 94 goals and collected three First Division titles and appeared in five FA Cup Finals. A very quick right winger, Jock was capped for his country during the 1903-04 season at the age of 19. After almost twelve seasons at Newcastle, Jock moved to Arsenal aged 29 in 1913 and played another 323 games and didn't retire till he was 42.

Alan Shearer – Wallsend Boys' Club

Born in Gosforth, Alan developed his skills at Wallsend Boys' Club before signing for Southampton. He left the Saints to join Blackburn Rovers where he helped them win the League title in 1995. He joined Newcastle United a year later for a then world record £15 million fee and over the next ten seasons became the club's all-time record goal scorer with 206 goals. Voted the Premier Leagues player of the decade, he is also the competition's top scorer with a total of 260 goals. Alan was a runner-up in the Premier League with the Magpies and reached two FA Cup Finals. He was capped 63 times for England scoring 30 goals and was captain of both United and his country for much of his stay at St James' Park. Alan collected the 'Footballer of the Year' and 'Player of the Year' awards three times before retiring in 2006.

Alan Thompson – Bolton Wanderers.

Jock Rutherford – Newcastle and Arsenal.

Peter Beardsley – Wallsend Boys' Club
Born in Longbenton, Peter joined Carlisle United from Wallsend Boys' Club before moving to Vancouver Whitecaps. He joined Newcastle in 1983 and made 326 appearances scoring 119 goals. He left to join Liverpool in 1987 where he won two League titles and an FA Cup, before moving to Everton and then returning to Newcastle in 1993. Peter was capped for England 59 times and scored 9 goals. After leaving St James' for a second time, he played for Bolton, Fulham and Hartlepool before retiring in 1999. He is currently reserve team coach at Newcastle.

Left: Peter Beardley running onto the pitch at Roker Park for the visit of Liverpool. Behind him is Barry Venison and Jan Molby.

Fraser Foster – Wallsend Boys' Club
Born at Hexham in 1988, Fraser joined Celtic from Newcastle United and won his first England cap against Chile in 2013.

Christine Hutchinson – Wallsend Ladies
Brought up in Wallsend, Christine played for Wallsend Ladies and made her England debut against Switzerland on 28th April 1977 and went on to win 10 caps in an illustrious international career.

Above: Fraser Forster – Southampton and England goalkeeper. Signed from Celtic for £10 million in 2014.

Left: Christine Hutchinson (left) with Jack Charlton and teammate Bernadette Tutte.

ENGLAND 'B' INTERNATIONALS

Steve Bruce
Manchester United and Wallsend Boys' Club

Steve Watson
Newcastle United and Wallsend Boys' Club

Right: Steve Bruce.

Far right: Steve Watson, Newcastle United, 1989-1998. Appearance: 208. Goals 12.

UNDER 21s / 23s INTERNATIONALS *

Ray Hankin
Leeds United and Wallsend Boys' Club

Gordon Nisbet
West Bromich Albion and Willington Quay Boys' Club

Lee Clark
Newcastle United and Wallsend Boys' Club

Neil McDonald
Newcastle United and Wallsend Boys' Club

Graeme Fenton
Aston Villa and Wallsend Boys' Club

(* the age requirement was changed in 1976)

Neil McDonald – Newcastle and later assistant manager at West Ham.

Ray Hankin while playing for Burnley.

Lee Clark – Newcastle, Sunderland and Fulham.

ENGLAND SCHOOLBOY INTERNATIONALS, UNDER 15s / 16s

Henry Chambers	Capped, 1911
Steve Howie	Capped, 1967
Neil McDonald	Capped, 1981
Lee Clark	Capped, 1987
Mark Maley	Capped, 1996
Adam Campbell	Capped, 2011

ENGLAND SCHOOLBOY INTERNATIONALS, UNDER 18s

Eric Steele	Capped, 1972
Mark Simpson	Capped, 1996
Steve Young	Capped, 1998
David Borley	Capped, 2001

ENGLAND BOYS' CLUBS INTERNATIONALS

Kenny Cramman	Capped, 1966
Billy Lisgoe	Capped, 1973
Michael Carrick	Capped, 1996

GREAT BRITAIN UNIVERSITIES

Greg Young	Capped, 2003

Steve Howie with England under 15s schoolboy cap.

Adam Campbell – England under 16s.

Mark Maley – England schoolboy under 15s international, 1996.

Steven Young – England under 18s schoolboy international.

Bill Lisgo – England Boys' Clubs, 1972.

Greg Young – British Universities international, 2003.

Michael Carrick with his England Boys' Club International under 16s cap in 1996.

CUP WINNERS AND FOOTBALL LEAGUE PLAYERS

CHAMPIONS LEAGUE WINNERS

Michael Carrick is the proud owner of a Champions League Winners Medal. He played in the Manchester United side that beat Chelsea in the 2008 final. He also played in the United side that lost to Barcelona at Wembley in the 2009 Final.

Alan Waddle was an unused substitute in the Liverpool squad for the 1977 final (then called the European Cup) against Borussia Monchengladbach.

Michael Carrick with the Champions League Trophy.

Michael Carrick's Champions League Winners medal, 2008.

Alan Waddle – Liverpool.

WALLSEND PLAYERS WITH PREMIER OR FIRST DIVISON TITLES

Jock Rutherford	3 titles in the early 1900s with Newcastle United
Frank Cuggy	1 title in 1913 with Sunderland
Sharkey Chambers	2 titles in the 1920s with Liverpool
Albert Stubbins	1 title in 1947 with Liverpool
Peter Beardsley	2 titles in 1980s with Liverpool
Steve Bruce	3 titles with Manchester United
Michael Carrick	5 titles with Manchester United

SCOTTISH LEAGUE CHAMPIONS

Alan Thompson	4 titles between 2000-2007 with Celtic
Fraser Foster	3 titles 2011-12, 2012-13, 2013-14 with Celtic

EUROPEAN CUP WINNERS CUP

Steve Bruce was part of the Manchester United team that defeated Barcelona in the 1991 Final.

FA CUP WINNERS

Jack Surtees, the former Willington Athletic centre forward, played for Sheffield Wednesday in their 1935 victory over West Bromich Albion.

Peter Beardsley was part of the Liverpool team that defeated Everton in the 1989 Final.

Steve Bruce won three winners medals with Manchester United in 1990, 1994, 1996, when they beat Crystal Palace, Chelsea and Liverpool in the finals.

Jock Rutherford was in the Newcastle United side that lifted the trophy in 1910 when they beat Barnsley in the final. He was also on the losing side for United in four finals.

Jack Roscamp, formerly of Wallsend AFC, scored twice in Blackburn's 3-1 win over Huddersfield in 1928.

Charlie Crowe, who played for St Luke's in the 1940s, was in the Newcastle side that beat Blackpool 2-0 in the 1951 final.

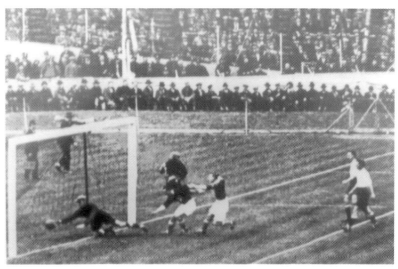
Jack Roscamp (dark strip) scores for Blackburn Rovers in the 3-1 FA Cup Final victory over Huddersfield Town.

Joe Harvey, holding the FA Cup, is lifted on to the shoulders of Frank Brennan and Jackie Milburn after Newcastle's Wembley victory in 1951. Former St Luke's player, Charlie Crowe, is 4th from the left with his arm around Ernie Taylor.

FOOTBALL LEAGUE CUP

Brian Laws.

Brian Laws was on the winning side twice with Nottingham Forest, beating Luton Town in the 1989 final and Oldham Athletic in 1990.

Steve Bruce was in the Manchester United side that lifted the trophy in 1992 beating Nottingham Forest in the final. He was also in the Norwich team that beat Sunderland in the 1985 final.

Graeme Fenton, the former Wallsend Boys Club player, was in the Aston Villa team that beat Manchester United in the 1994 final at Wembley. Graeme was also voted man of the match.

FA AMATEUR CUP

Tony Cassidy became the only Wallsend born player to claim a FA Amateur Cup Winners medal when he was part of the North Shields team that lifted the trophy in 1969, beating Sutton United 2-1 in front of a 47,000 crowd at Wembley Stadium.

Right: North Shield FC after victory at Wembley in the FA Amateur Cup with Tony Cassidy seen holding the plinth.

FA VASE

Three former Wallsend Boys' Club players were involved in the Whitley Bay 2-0 FA Vase victory over Glossop North End at Wembley Stadium in 2009.

Left: Whitley Bay FC celebrate winning the FA Vase at Wembley. Lee Picton is right front row, Chris Bone fourth from right back row and coach Gavin Fell is second from left back row, with the jesters hat on.

Ex-Marine Park midfield player Richie Percy was on the losing side at Wembley Stadium in the 1979-80 FA Vase Final when Guisborough Town lost 0-2 to Stamford.

Left: Richie Percy with his FA Vase Runners-up medal, while playing for Guisborough Town, 1979-80.

FA YOUTH CUP

Former Corinthians Juniors goalkeeper Stan Craig was between the sticks when Newcastle United Juniors lifted the trophy by beating Wolves 2-1 on aggregate in 1962.

Former Boys' Club players Jeff Wrightson, Ian Bogie and Paul Stephenson were part of the Newcastle squad that won the cup in 1985 defeating Watford 4-1 in the final.

Michael Carrick was in the West Ham United team that won the cup in 1999 by beating Coventry City 9-0 on aggregate, which is a record Youth Cup Final score.

Newcastle United FA Youth Cup Winners, 1962. Stan Craig, goalkeeper, is in the back row.

Right: Newcastle United Juniors, Youth Cup Winners, 1985. Back row: Suggett, Kilford, Wrightson, Tinnion, Allon, Kelly, Forster, Scott, Nelson. Front row: Stephenson, Hayton, Harbach, Dickinson, Gascione, Bogie, Nesbit, McKenzie.

FA TROPHY

Chris Moore was part of the Darlington team that lifted the trophy in 2010 beating Mansfield Town 1-0 at Wembley. Chris played his early football with Wallsend Boys' Club.

WALLSEND PLAYERS WHO BECOME MANAGERS

	Club	Clubs Managed
Steve Bruce	Wallsend Boys' Club	Sheffield United, Huddersfield, Wigan Crystal Palace, Birmingham City Sunderland, Hull City
Brian Laws	Wallsend Boys' Club	Grimsby Town
Lee Clark	Wallsend Boys' Club	Huddersfield Town, Birmingham City
Alan Shearer	Wallsend Boys' Club	Newcastle United
Frank Cuggy	Bigges Main Celtic	Celta Vigo
Graham Carr	Corinthians	Northampton Town

ASSISTANT MANAGERS, FIRST TEAM COACHES

	Club	Clubs Managed
Neil McDonald	Wallsend Boys' Club	West Ham
Albert Stubbins	Bigges Main Celtic	USA National Team
Alan Thompson	Wallsend Boys' Club	Celtic

WALLSEND PLAYERS WHO HAVE PLAYED IN THE NEWCASTLE UNITED FIRST TEAM

	Club	Signed
A. Mowatt	Wallsend Park Villa	1896
W. Innead	Wallsend Park Villa	1900
O. Richardson	Wallsend Park Villa	1902
J.P. McClarence	Wallsend Park Villa	1904
T Lowes	Wallsend Park Villa	1910
T. Hughes	Wallsend Park Villa	1912
J. Lockey	Willington Athletic	1895
T. Barlett	Willington Athletic	1896
J. Rutherford	Willington Athletic	1902
J. Ridley	Willington Athletic	1907
S. Spike	Willington Athletic	1940
R. Rutherford	St Luke's	1944
G. Luke	St Luke's	1950
B. McKinney	St Luke's	1956
J.G. Scott	Wallsend Slipway	1910
N.H. Tapken	Wallsend Thermal	1933
S. Barber	Wallsend FC	1925
C.T. Booth	Wallsend Elm Villa	1913
W.B. Foster	Howdon British Legion	1932
D.J. Robinson	Wallsend Boys' Club	1986
D. Roche	Wallsend Boys' Club	1986
P. Beardsley	Wallsend Boys' Club	1983
J.G. Wrightson	Wallsend Boys' Club	1985
I. Bogie	Wallsend Boys' Club	1985
P. Stephenson	Wallsend Boys' Club	1985
A. Lormor	Wallsend Boys' Club	1987
A. Thompson	Wallsend Boys' Club	1989
J. Watson	Wallsend Boys' Club	1989
S. Watson	Wallsend Boys' Club	1990
A. Shearer	Wallsend Boys' Club	1996
A. Stubbins	North Shields Athletic	1936
A. Campbell	Wallsend Boys' Club	2013
C. Hedworth	Wallsend Boys' Club	1984
E. Cook	Wallsend AFC	1919
D. Lackenby	Wallsend Schools	1962

Alan Shearer – Newcastle United number 9.

Peter Beardsley – Newcastle, Liverpool, Everton and England.

WALLSEND PLAYERS WHO HAVE PLAYED LEAGUE FOOTBALL

	Club	League Club Played For
S. Henderson	Howdon British Legion	1920s Chelsea
D. Lawson	Willington Quay & Howdon BC	1970s Everton
A. Waddle	Wallsend Boys' Club	1980s Liverpool
H. Chambers	Rosehill Villa	1920s Liverpool
B. Scott	Willington Athletic	1930s Brentford
J. Hedley	Willington	1950s Sunderland
F. Cuggy	Willington Athletic	1910 Sunderland
S. Cuggy	Willington Athletic	1910 Hull City
G. Talbot	Unknown	1920s Liverpool
B. Henderson	Howdon British Legion	1920s Blackpool
M. Carrick	Wallsend Boys' Club	2000s Manchester United
S. Bruce	Wallsend Boys' Club	1990s Manchester United
J. Surtees	Willington Athletic	1930s Sheffield Wednesday
G. Nisbet	Willington Quay & Howdon BC	1970s West Brom
J. Ingham	Wallsend Boys' Club	1950s Gateshead
D. Taylor	Wallsend Boys' Club	2012 Oldham Athletic
P. Baker	Wallsend Boys' Club	1990s Carlisle United
D. Bobley	Wallsend Boys' Club	1990s Bury
V. Chapman	Wallsend Boys' Club	1980s Huddersfield
T. Dinning	Wallsend Boys' Club	1990s Wolves
N. Evans	Wallsend Boys' Club	1990s Brighton
F. Foster	Wallsend Boys' Club	2014 Southampton
R. Hankin	Wallsend Boys' Club	1980s Leeds United
S. Baker	Wallsend Boys' Club	1980s Southampton
M. Bridges	Wallsend Boys' Club	1990s Leeds United
D. Bukowski	Wallsend Boys' Club	1970s Northampton
P. Cavener	Wallsend Boys' Club	1970s Burnley
G. Fenton	Wallsend Boys' Club	1990s Blackburn
D. Gray	Wallsend Boys' Club	2010 Hibernian
R. Hindmarsh	Wallsend Boys' Club	1980s Wolves
N. Hooks	Wallsend Boys' Club	1970s Notts County
S. Hutchinson	Wallsend Boys' Club	2000s Motherwell
R. Irving	Wallsend Boys' Club	1960s Ipswich
B. Laws	Wallsend Boys' Club	1980s Notts Forest
G. Leonard	Wallsend Boys' Club	1970s West Brom

Jack Sibbald, formerly with Elm Villa, 2nd from right, back row, pictured with Brentford in 1912.

Jack Hedley playing for Sunderland in the 1950s.

K. Lockhart	Wallsend Boys' Club	1970s	Burnley
M. Maley	Wallsend Boys' Club	2000s	Sunderland
K. McDonald	Wallsend Boys' Club	2000s	Hibernian
K. McGarrigle	Wallsend Boys' Club	1990s	Brighton
M. Nash	Wallsend Boys' Club	1980s	Darlington
D. Parker	Wallsend Boys' Club	1970s	Burnley
P. Ray	Wallsend Boys' Club	1970s	Burnley
T. Sealey	Wallsend Boys' Club	1970s	Southampton
K. Smith	Wallsend Boys' Club		Cambridge United
P. Tait	Wallsend Boys' Club	1990s	Wigan Athletic
D. Walker	Wallsend Boys' Club	1970s	Burnley
M. Wardrobe	Wallsend Boys' Club	1970s	Burnley
T. Widdrington	Wallsend Boys' Club	1990s	Southampton
J. Wrightson	Wallsend Boys' Club	1990s	Preston
B. Pringle	Wallsend Boys' Club	2000s	Derby
B. Richardson	Wallsend Boys' Club	1970s	Notts Forest
E. Steele	Wallsend Boys' Club	1980s	Derby
J. Tate	Wallsend Boys' Club	1970s	Burnley
L. Taylor	Wallsend Boys' Club	1980s	Watford
M. Smith	Wallsend Boys' Club	2014	Swindon
B. Wardrobe	Wallsend Boys' Club	1970s	Sunderland
I. Watson	Wallsend Boys' Club	1970s	Sunderland
B. Wright	Wallsend Boys' Club	1980s	Burnley
C. Elliott	Wallsend Boys' Club	2014	Partick Thistle
D. Taylor	Wallsend Boys' Club	2013	Oldham Athletic
N. Call	Corinthians	1960s	Brighton
T. Winship	Wallsend Park Villa	1920s	Arsenal
J. Sibbald	Wallsend Elm Villa	1911	Brentford
B. Front	Wallsend Elm Villa	1911	Brentford
J. Allen	Wallsend AFC	1910	Crystal Palace
J. Rawlinson	Corinthians	1960s	Bury
J. Roscamp	Wallsend AFC	1920s	Blackburn
H. Harvey	Wallsend AFC	1920s	Cardiff City
J. Scott	Wallsend AFC	1920s	Liverpool
J. Patterson	Wallsend AFC	1920s	Arsenal
H. O'Niel	Wallsend AFC	1920s	Sheffield Wednesday
F. McKenna	Wallsend AFC	1920s	Middlesbrough
B. Mullen	Wallsend AFC	1930	Hartlepool
S. Cuggy	Cramlington Jnrs	1990s	Maidstone United

David Lawson – Transferred from Huddersfield to Everton for a then record transfer fee for a goalkeeper of £85,000 in 1972.

Gordon Nisbet – West Bromwich Albion, 1972.

Tony Sealy – former Wallsend Boys Club player who played for Southampton in the 1979 League Cup Final.

WALLSEND TEAMS

WALLSEND TEAMS OPERATING IN 1911-12

Willington Athletic
Wallsend Park Villa
Wallsend Collieries
Howdon St Paul's
Wallsend White Star
Wallsend Camp Villa
Wallsend Parkside
Wallsend Hope Villa
Wallsend North End
Wallsend United
Wallsend IOGT
Wallsend Gladstone Villa
Wallsend St Joseph's
Wallsend Alexandria
Wallsend Black Watch
Wallsend Caledonians
Wallsend Slipway
Wallsend St Columba's (3 teams)
Wallsend West End
Bigges Main Excelsior
Wallsend Elm Villa
Howdon FC
Wallsend British Legion
Howdon East End
Wallsend St George's
Wallsend Alba
Neptune Villa
Howdon Dock
Willington FC
Wallsend Athletic Reserves
Wallsend Springwell Villa
Willington Royal Oak FC
Willington United (2 teams)
Wallsend Leslie Villa
Willington Bewick
Wallsend Neptune Villa
Willington Royal Rovers
Howden Tyne View
Wallsend Argyle
Wallsend Rising Sun
Wallsend Curzon Villa
Wallsend Angus Villa
St Christopher's

Willington Athletic Reserves
Wallsend Amateurs
Wallsend Colliery's Reserves
Willington UM
Wallsend Blue Star
Wallsend Royal
Wallsend Kingdom Villa
Wallsend Elton
Wallsend Presbyterians
Wallsend United Reserves
Point Pleasant
Wallsend PT
Carville Albion
Wallsend Lesh Villa
Wallsend Hope Villa
Rosehill Villa
Wallsend St Peter's
Wallsend Park Albion
Wallsend Excelsior
Willington North End
Willington St Aidan's
Rosehill Hillside
Wallsend East End
Wallsend Athletic
Wallsend Lawson Villa
Wallsend Royal Oak
Wallsend Victoria
Willington Wednesday
Wallsend Primitive Methodists
Wallsend BLB
Davis St Mission
Wallsend Coach Rovers
Howdon Adelaide
Wallsend Nelson Villa
Willington St Mary's
Bigges Main Celtic
Bigges Main 'A'
Willington Presbyterians
Vine Street Wanderers
Park Road Wesleyans
Burn Closes
Howdon Amateurs

Eighty-five sides – An incredible number when you compare it with now, a century later we have six senior Saturday teams playing.

On the facing page is a copy of the Wallsend & District League of 1912-13 which has three divisions!

Wallsend & District League 1st Div, 1912-13

	P	W	L	D	PTS
Wallsend St Columba's	4	4	0	0	8
Howdon East End	3	3	0	0	6
Jarrow Brinkburn	5	2	3	0	4
Jarrow Royal Oak	3	1	1	1	3
Jarrow Adelaide	4	1	2	1	3
Wallsend Coach Rovers	1	1	0	0	2
Wallsend Colliery A	3	1	2	0	2
Davis St Mission	4	1	3	0	2
Willington United	1	0	1	0	1

Wallsend & District League 2nd Div, 1912-13

	P	W	L	D	PTS
Howdon Adelaide	7	6	1	0	12
Jarrow Celtic	7	5	1	1	11
Willington Royal Oak	7	5	1	1	11
Wallsend Elton Villa	8	5	2	1	11
Wallsend Carville	8	5	2	1	11
Pelaw Argyle	7	3	1	3	9
Wallsend Black Watch	4	3	0	1	7
Bigges Main Celtic	7	3	3	1	7
Wallsend St Columba's	6	2	2	2	6
Wallsend East End	6	3	3	0	6
Wallsend Blue Star	7	3	4	0	6
Willington Bewicke	5	2	2	1	5
Willington Nelson Villa	6	2	3	1	5
Hebburn St Cuthbert's	6	2	3	1	5
Heworth United	6	2	3	1	5
Wallsend Neptune Villa	3	1	1	1	3
Hebburn Adelaide	2	0	0	2	2
Hebburn Rose Villa	6	1	5	0	2
Willington Royal Rovers	4	0	3	1	1
Howdon Tyne View	1	0	1	0	0
Hebburn North End	3	0	3	0	0
Jarrow St Peter's	4	0	4	0	0
Wallsend Argyle	5	0	5	0	0
Hebburn Celtic	0	0	0	0	0
Wallsend Rising Sun	0	0	0	0	0

Wallsend & District League 3rd Div, 1912-13

	P	W	L	D	PTS
Wallsend West End	7	5	0	2	12
Wallsend Carville	7	5	1	1	11
Wallsend Springwell	7	5	1	1	11
Colliery Juniors	5	4	0	1	9
Willington United	5	4	1	0	8
Byker Cresswell	6	4	2	0	8
Wallsend St Columba's	8	3	4	1	7
Wallsend Leslie Villa	6	3	3	0	6
Wallsend Albion	6	2	3	1	5
Walsend Curzon Villa	6	1	4	1	3
Walker Angus Villa	5	1	3	1	3
Bigges Main Celtic A	4	1	3	0	2
Walker Diamond Villa	1	1	0	0	2
Walker Villa A	2	0	2	0	0
Willington St Mary's	3	1	2	0	0
Walker Primrose	5	0	5	0	0
Willington Royal Oak A	2	0	2	0	0
Hebburn Celtic A	0	0	0	0	0

WILLINGTON ATHLETIC AND WILLINGTON ATHLETIC RESERVES

Leagues: Northern Alliance / Northern Amateur / Tyneside Alliance

Northern Alliance Champions	1899-1900, 1904-05, 1905-06, 1909-10
Northumberland Senior Cup winners	1895-96, 1896-97
Northumberland Senior Cup runners up	1901-02, 1910-11
Northumberland Challenge Bowl winners	1890-91, 1891-92, 1905-06
Tyneside Charity Shield	1890-91 (Beat Newcastle East End 1-0 in the Final
Northern Amateur League Div 2 Champions	1934-35
Northumberland Amateur Cup Winners	1938-39

Secretaries: P. Bagnall, 1930s. Mr E. Scott, 1912.

Club Colours: Blue.

Perhaps one of the strongest teams Wallsend has ever produced, they played in four Northumberland Senior Cup Finals around the turn of the twentieth century and were champions of the very strong Northern Alliance around the same period. However, the continual loss of their top players who moved on for more money elsewhere and the outbreak of both world wars had a massive effect on the club. They folded at the outbreak of the First War in 1914 and although they reformed in 1919, they were never the team they once were.

Willington Athletic, 1904-05 – Northern Alliance Champions and Tynemouth Infirmary Cup. Back row: Woodman, Wright, Charlton, McLarney, Lavers, Morris, McDonald, Kaley, Wanless, Bewick. Middle row: Anderson, Barras, Hewitt, Brown, Rutherford, Gilchrist, Chambers. Front: Harrison, Shields.

They folded for good just after the outbreak of the Second World War. On the 30th October 1898, a crowd of 6,000 saw Newcastle United beat Willington Athletic 6-0 in the FA Cup 3rd qualifying round with goals from Allen 4, Campbell and Jordon.

Left: Willington Athletic in the 1930s – Northern Amateur League. Back row: Committee. Third row: R. Slack, E. Hopkins, B. Wilson, Jock WIlmott, J. Boardman. Middle row: Trainer R. Porter, J. Tomaselli, R. Simpson, J. Ford, Secretary P. Bagnall. Sitting: W. Waterworth, J. Jamison, G. Atchinson, E. Wilkinson, S. Smoult. Front: F. Ryan, G. Hunter, H. Stott.

Willington Athletic appeared in four Northumberland Senior Cup Final:

1896 at St James' Park

Willington Athletic 3   Wallsend Park Villa 0
(Barlett, Cumings, Lamb)

1897 at St James' Park, attendance 5,000

Willington Athletic 3   Shankhouse 0
(Lamb 2, Barlett)

1902 at St James' Park

Willington Athletic 0   Wallsend Park Villa 3
                                    (Barnfather 2, Shields)

1911 at St James' Park

Willington Athletic 0   Newcastle United Res 6

Right: A newspaper cutting for the Northumberland Senior Cup Final of 1897.

FOOTBALL EDITION.

7.0 P.M.

TO-DAY'S FOOTBALL.

ASSOCIATION.

NORTHUMBERLAND SENIOR CUP FINAL.

SHANKHOUSE v. WILLINGTON ATHLETIC.

CONTEST AT ST. JAMES'S PARK.

POSITIONS.

SHANKHOUSE.
Goal: Ord.
Backs: R. Robson and A. Patten.
Half-backs: J. Forster, T. Rendall, and C. Ritson.
Forwards: Hedley, Willis, Hume, Gibson, and Briggs.

O

Forwards: Bartlett, Simpson, McLucas, Cummings, and Lamb.
Half-backs: Bonner, Rice, and Sproul.
Backs: A. Bell and J. Bell.
Goal: T. Mason.
WILLINGTON ATHLETIC.

Referee: Mr. A. H. White, Newcastle.

Newspaper Report
Northern Alliance, 1896
Willington Athletic 4 Sunderland 3

Though the weather was wet and disagreeable there was still a good gathering of spectators as the Rosehill ground to witness this game. Playing up the hill in the first half, the home team managed to hold their own, and when the whistle sounded for the interval each side had scored once. On resuming Sunderland showed some excellent combination but in front of goal Willington proved very dangerous their fine shooting eventually pulling them through.

Newspaper Report
Northern Alliance, 1896
Willington Athletic 8 Hebburn Argyle 0

Yesterday, at Rosehill, this Alliance fixture came off in the presence of a fair number of spectators. Argyle played one man short. Willington did all the pressing and shot after shot was send in amidst the enthusiasm of the onlookers, It was quite evident from the first that Argyle was outmatched for before the game was fifteen minutes old, Bartlett, Lamb, Weatherburn and Rice had each scored a goal for the homesters. Before the whistle blew they had added another goal to their score, which at this time stood at five to nothing. During the second half Willington followed up their advantage, and three more goals were scored for them, through Rice, Weatherburn and Lamb. A very one sided game ended all in favour of the home team.

Right: The Northern Alliance Championship Trophy won by Willington on four occasions.

A cartoon showing Willington v Morpeth, 1909.

Northern Alliance, final table, 1909

	P	W	L	D	F	A	Pts
Blyth Spartans	28	17	3	8	70	21	42
Byker East End	28	17	8	3	60	36	37
Blaydon United	28	14	6	8	55	31	36
Newburn	28	13	7	8	58	40	34
Mickley	28	13	9	6	43	38	32
Ashington	28	12	10	6	56	50	30
Bedlington U	28	11	9	8	42	50	30
Walker Parish	28	10	9	9	46	42	29
Annfield Celtic	28	12	13	3	42	49	27
Willington Ath	28	8	10	10	37	43	26
Morpeth Harriers	27	8	12	7	42	52	23
Newcastle E.E.	28	8	17	2	32	53	20
Scotswood	28	8	17	3	43	63	19
Kingston Villa	26	8	18	2	38	65	18

Players that went on to play league football

J. Lockey	Newcastle United	1895	T. Barlett	Newcastle United	1896
J. Rutherford	Newcastle United	1902	N. Brown	Sunderland	1904
J. Ridley	Newcastle United	1907	S. Spike	Newcastle United	1939
B. Scott	Brentford	1933	J. Surtees	Sheffield Wed	1933
F. Cuggy	Sunderland	1909			

J. Surtees played in the FA Cup Final win over West Brom in 1935.

WALLSEND PARK VILLA / WALLSEND AFC

Leagues: Northern Alliance / North Eastern League/ Tyneside League   1890s

Northern Alliance	Champions	1903-04
Poor Children's Holiday Cup	Winners	1894-95
Northumberland Minor Cup	Winners	1894-95
Northumberland Senior Cup	Winners	1901-02
Northumberland Senior Cup	Runners-up	1895-96, 1904-05, 1906-07, 1929-30
Gateshead Charity Cup	Winners	1900-01
Northumberland Challenge Bowl	Winners	1903-04, 1906-07, 1929-30
Newcastle Infirmary Cup	Winners	1908-09
Tynemouth Infirmary Cup	Runners-up	1929-30
Tyneside Charity Shield	Winners	1929-30
North Eastern League	Runners-up	1927-28
Northumberland Aged Miners' Cup	Winners	1933-34

Grounds: Benton Way, North Road.
Manager: F. Cuggy, 1921-23.
Club President: J. Wipea, 1890-1914.

Right: Wallsend Park Villa, Gateshead Charity Cup, 1900. Back row: J. Miller, D. McGill, J. Wiper, R. Arnott, J. Clark, W. Thompson, W. Donald, E. Childs, E. Rowan, Clough. Middle row: T. Maxwell, R. Fyfe, A. Scaife. Front row: J. Neil, H. Dale, R. Ward, W. Heward, T. Rowan.

Tyneside League, 1896.	P	W	L	D	F	A	P
Wallsend Park Villa	15	9	4	2	50	33	20
Leadgate Park	10	8	2	0	40	13	16
St Peter's Albion	11	5	2	4	36	23	14
Hobson Wanderers	11	6	4	1	33	19	13
Mickley	9	5	2	2	29	14	12
Hexham Excelsior	8	4	3	1	19	21	9
Wallsend Celtic	10	2	5	3	22	27	7
Prudhoe	9	2	6	1	18	30	5
Gateshead Engineers	12	1	9	2	9	50	4
Gateshead St Cuthberts	7	1	6	0	13	29	2

Players that played league football

A. Mowatt	Newcastle United	1891
W. Inneard	Newcastle United	1902
A. Richardson	Newcastle United	1902
J.P. McClarence	Newcastle United	1904
T. Lowes	Newcastle United	1910
B.S. Barber	Newcastle United	1925
T. Hughes	Newcastle United	1912
J. Cavannah	Clapton Orient	1910
T. Winship	Arsenal	1911
J. Allen	Crystal Palace	1924
B Mullen	Hartlepool	1930

Right: Tom Hughes. A former Wallsend Park Villa player, Tom was transferred to Newcastle United in 1911 for an £80 fee and made two appearances in the first team. He volunteered to join the army at the outbreak of hostilities in 1914 and was killed in action at Ypres in 1915.

Wallsend appeared in five Northumberland Senior Cup Finals being successful on only one occasion.

1896 at St James' Park	Wallsend Park Villa 0	Willington Athletic 3
1902 at St James' Park	Wallsend Park Villa 3 (Barnfather 2, Shields)	Willington Athletic 0
1907 at Hawkeys Lane North Shields, (Attendance 6,000)	Wallsend Park Villa 1 (Miller)	Newcastle United Res 4 (Higgins 2, Harding 2)
1905 at St James' Park (Attendance 5,500)	Wallsend Park Villa 1 (Barron)	Newcastle United Res 2 (Tindesley, Thompson)
1930 at St James' Park (Attendance 6,500)	Wallsend AFC 1 (Grieve)	Newcastle United Res 3 (Chalmers, McCurley, Scott)

Wallsend Park Villa lifted the Newcastle Infirmary Cup at St James' Park in 1909 by beating:

1st Round	Kingston Villa	4-0	2nd Round	Jarrow FC	3-0
3rd Round	Sunderland West End	2-1	Semi-final	Washington United	5-2
Final	North Shields Athletic	2-1			

Park Villa were one of Northumberland's big teams at the turn of the twentieth century and after a lot of early success turned semi-professional in the 1908-09 season and joined the North Eastern League. In 1912 Villa changed their name to Wallsend AFC and in 1921 England International Frank Cuggy signed from Sunderland as player manager on a two year contract. The club enjoyed limited success in the league and by 1922 the financial problems had started. With a wage bill of £52 per week and a ground rental of £200 per year which they found a crippling amount, falling gates and the start of the depression with 6,000 men out of work in Wallsend alone, games that season were not attracting enough support to cover the costs – although the Newcastle Reserves fixture brought in a gate of £265 for a midweek game and the Sunderland Reserves game £161. The gates began to plummet and although the supporters club continued to raise cash and the directors dug deep into their own pockets the club began the long road into decline and finally went under in 1937.

Right: Wallsend AFC's fixtures for the 1930-31 season. Note the amount of travelling the club had to do and the fact that they had fixtures on the 25th, 26th and 27th of December! The result of the Tynemouth Infirmary Cup Final played at Appleby Park, North Shields on 1st September was: Wallsend 2 Walker Celtic 3.

Right: Wallsend Park Villa, 1909. Tom Winship, extreme right middle row, went on to play for Arsenal from 1910 to 1926.

Left: Wallsend AFC, 1920-21. Back row: T. Clark (trainer), W. Quinn, G. Harrison (director), P. Mahon, A. Hogg, T. Oxley (director), R. Parker, E. Smith, G. Newman (manager). Front row: E. Lumsden, J. KcKenna, J. Roscamp, T. Pearson, F. Cuggy, F. McKenna, J. Clark.

POINT PLEASANT ROVERS

League: Tyneside Alliance

Ground: Point Pleasant.

On 7th January 1888, Newcastle East End just before their name change to Newcastle United met Point Pleasant in the Northumberland & Durham FA Challenge Cup. East End running out 19-0 winners which is still a Newcastle United record victory.

Right: Point Pleasant Rovers, 1913.

WATERFORD FC

Newcastle & District League 1896

This photograph was taken in Wallsend Burn which suggests they played on the hospital field. The name – Waterford FC – also suggests that they may have been a group of Irish men who had settled in Wallsend.

Left: Waterford FC, 1890s.

Newcastle & District League, 1896

	P	W	D	L	F	A	Pts
Waterford	10	5	3	2	25	18	13
Mickley Reserve	9	4	3	2	25	11	11
Heaton Science and Art	9	5	1	3	17	10	11
Scotswood Ord	8	5	1	2	13	11	11
Benton Square Albion	7	4	1	2	14	8	9
Brighton	11	4	0	7	17	23	8
Walbottle	7	3	1	3	13	19	7
Worswick Rovers	6	1	0	5	9	18	2
Throckley EMS	5	0	0	5	3	18	0

WALLSEND COLLIERY EXCELSIOR

Northern Amateur League Division 2 — Runners-up 1910-11
Northumberland Minor Cup — Winners 1912-13
Northumberland Amateur League Cup — Winners 1912-13

Ground: North Road, 1912.

Right: Wallsend Collierys, 1908. John Grieves is 5th left, back row.

HADRIAN UM

Photograph taken by the water pump in Wallsend Burn in 1914.

League: unknown.

WALLSEND CONGREGATION

League: United Free Churches   1909   Ground: unknown.

United Free Churches Amateur League Division I – final table, 1909

	P	W	L	D	F	A	P
Dilston Wesleyan	23	19	2	2	64	22	40
Bainbridge Mem	23	18	3	2	71	36	38
Fife Street Guild	22	15	4	3	42	24	33
Pelaw United Ch	22	9	7	6	40	32	24
Wallsend Congre	22	8	8	6	30	31	22
Derby St Guild	22	9	10	3	33	41	21
Benwell Press Ch	22	8	10	4	29	32	20
Wingrove Presby	22	7	10	5	41	41	19
Wallsend Met Ch	22	8	12	2	51	42	18
East End Mission	22	5	13	4	24	38	14
St Paul's Congre	22	4	16	2	19	29	10
Shieldfield Ad S	22	3	18	1	8	85	7

Dilston Beat Bainbridge in a deciding match

ST CHRISTOPHER'S

Church of England League   1912   Ground: unknown.

HOWDON WANDERERS

Tyneside Alliance League   1902   Ground: unknown.

HOWDON AMATEURS

Northern Amateur League   1909   Ground: unknown.

WALLSEND AMATEURS

Northern Amateur League   Champions 1910-11
Northern Amateur League Cup   Winners   1909-10, 1910-11
Wallsend & District League   1962

Ground: unknown, 1911, St Peter's Road, 1963.

A second Wallsend Amateurs played in the Wallsend & District League in the 1962-63 season. Made up of employees of Wallsend Council, they only lasted a couple of seasons.

Right: Wallsend Amateurs, 1961. Back row: J. Bell, G. Ward, I. Milne, G. Holmes, P. Carey, G. Lowdon. Front row: J. Weddle, W. Noble, J. Cosgrove, J. Irving, A. Murison.

WALLSEND ELM VILLA

Northern Amateur League Cup   Winners   1905-06
Tyneside Alliance   1910-11
Willington Quay Nursing Cup   Winners   1908-09 shared
Northumberland Minor Cup   Winners   1910-11

Ground: The Avenue, North Road Ground.
Secretary: Mr Myhill, 1910.

Wallsend Elm Villa with Northumberland Minor Cup, 1910-11. Players and reserves include: Clark, Maxwell, Lake (goal keeper), Bell, Craig, Ferguson, W. Dobson, Neal, O'Neill, Smith, Taylor, Thompson, H. Dobson, Grant, Milne, Moody.

Photographed with the Minor Cup in 1911 and their own ground being built, Elm Villa seemed set for greater things but appeared to have folded about the time of the First World War.

Players who went on to play league football.

J. Sibbald	Brentford	1910
B. Front	Brentford	1910
C. Booth	Newcastle United	1913

Right: Curtis Booth, Elm Villa, joined Newcastle United in 1913 and played 42 games and scored 11 goals in a career interrupted by the war years before moving to Norwich City.

Tyneside League Final Table, 1911

	P	W	L	D	F	A	P
Windy Nook	28	21	3	4	76	27	46
Slipway	28	19	6	3	63	36	41
Wallsend Elm Villa	28	16	8	4	50	33	36
Felling ER	28	14	6	8	51	35	36
Pelaw	28	13	7	8	62	36	34
Boldon Colliery	28	15	10	3	43	36	33
Gateshead R	28	11	11	6	45	37	28
New York	28	12	12	4	44	49	28
Jarrow Blackett	28	11	11	6	38	49	28
Shields Albion	28	7	11	10	44	51	24
Gosforth	28	9	14	5	51	57	23
Boldon Villa	28	9	15	4	38	43	22
Hebburn BW	28	7	15	6	32	49	20
Jarrow Cald's	28	3	19	6	26	62	12
Willington SA	28	4	23	1	21	84	9

Newspaper Report

Wallsend Elm Villa 2 Wallsend Amateurs 0, 27th December 1907

These teams met in Northumberland Minor Cup tie on the former's ground on Saturday. There was a good gate. At the outset the Villans pressed and O'Hanlon was responsible for a fine effort. He transferred to Clark who put the leather over the bar. The homesters changed the venue and Finlay worked the leather into a good position and made an opening for Boardman, who had hard lines in not scoring, the ball grazing the crossbar. The Villans kept the Amateur defence busy for a while after this and Patterson succeeded in the opening scoring. As the interval approached the Amateurs tried hard to equalise, but the visitor's defence was too strong for them. On changing ends the game was fairly evenly contested, and the Villans were fortunate enough to further increase their score. Although the Amateurs made strenuous efforts to reduce the visitors lead they were unable to do so, the Villans putting up a very stout defence.

HOWDON ADULT SCHOOL

League: Tyneside Temperence   1912   Ground: unknown.

WILLINGTON UM

South Shields & District League   Champions   1908-09
Newcastle & District Amateur League   1911

Ground: Howdon Station.

Right: Willington Quay United – South Shields League Shield, 1909. Includes, back row: R. Foster, C. Humphrey, Marshal, E. Beatty, W. Radford, T. Marley, H. Finch, J. Scott. Second row: W. Fletcher, J. Batey, Gray, Cockburn, J. Wilkinson, J. Finch, J. Lofstadt, J. Spencer, A. Snowdon, T. Richardson, J. Stott. Third row: A. Wright, J. Stewart, C. Hedley, B. Wright, R. Stott, T. Rogers. Front row: R. Lofstadt, J. Campbell, W. Crosby, H. Morton, G. Beatty, J. Sample.

Shields & District League – final table, 1909

	P	W	L	D	F	A	Pts
Willington UM	26	20	1	5	77	16	45
Hebburn B.W	26	19	4	3	88	28	39
Jarrow Blackett	26	17	6	3	64	32	37
Boldon Villa	25	15	4	6	68	34	36
St Hilda	26	16	8	2	?	42	34
Empire	25	13	6	6	46	36	32
Olive Blossom	26	12	11	3	50	46	27
Shields Alb 'A'	25	5	10	10	40	54	20
Simonside	25	6	13	6	41	54	18
Jarrow St Bede	26	5	13	8	33	54	18
Boldon Albion	26	6	17	3	35	67	15
Murton Row Un	26	4	16	6	25	78	14

ROYAL OAK FC

Tyneside Alliance early 1900s

Ground: unknown.

Left: Wallsend Royal Oak FC – founder members of the Tyneside League. Hugh Lynch is 2nd from right, back row.

WALLSEND OLD BOYS' FC

Gateshead Church League
Gosforth & District League
Newcastle & District Church League

Established: 1906.   Colours: White shirts, blue shorts.   Secretary: Mr E. Dent.

HOWDON ST PAUL'S

Newcastle & District Church League   1909
Tyneside Church League   1910-11

Ground: unknown.

Howdon & Willington Quay St Paul's, 1909. Back row: Vicar J. Hughes, E. Scott, W. Heron, R. Blackwell, G. McDougall, J. Hindmarsh, J. Waugh, Mr Cowell, Mr Lawson, Mr Scott. Middle row: J. Balmer, T. Birtley, W. Wilson, J. Oats, B. Swan (President). Front row: A. Kirkley, G. Brown, J. Carney, W. Hill, S. Abott, S. Abbott, J. Smith.

HOWDON ST MARY'S

Tyneside Alliance League 1902

Ground: unknown.
Colours: Black and white stripes.

Right: St Mary's, 1918-19. Back row: C. Lavers, R. Sanders, W. Anderson, W. Young, S. Gray, W. Charlton. Front row: J. Kirsip, C. Gray, M. English, W. Clayton, J. Johnston.

ROSEHILL VILLA

Wallsend Charity Shield	Winners	1922-23
Northern Amateur League	Champions	1922-23, 1924-25
Northern Amateur League Cup	Winners	1923-24

Rosehill Villa was a top local side in the 1880s and '90s and regularly competed against the likes of Newcastle East End, Newcastle West End, Rendal etc. They continued as a top side until the mid-1930s. They ran a very successful junior team that won the Northumberland Junior Cup in 1910. Former player Henry 'Sharkey' Chambers went on to captain Liverpool and England in the 1920s.

Above: Rosehill Villa, 1908.

Left: Rosehill Villa, 1911. England international Sharkey Chambers is right of the player with the shield. W. Carson, J. Watson and goalkeeper Wilson are among the others.

WILLINGTON WEDNESDAY

Newcastle & District Business House Wednesday League
Northumberland FA Mid-week Challenge Cup   Winners 1911-12.

Willington Wednesday beat Newcastle Post Offices 1-0 in the final to lift the 1912 County Cup.

Ground: unknown.

ROSEHILL AMATEURS

Northern Amateur League, Division 2 Champions 1920-21

Ground: unknown.

WILLINGTON PRESBYTERIANS

Free Church League	1919
Shields & District league	1911

Ground: Rosehill.

WILLINGTON NORTH END

Members of the Northern Amateur League 1904-05
Willington Quay Nursing Cup Winners 1908-09
Tyneside League 1910-11

Ground: unknown.

Shared the Willington Quay Nursing Cup in 1909 after a 2-2 draw with the powerful Wallsend Elm Villa in the final.

Right: Willington North End, 1889. Back row includes: M. Long, W. Snowdon, T. Smith, T. Snowdon, T. Tully, J. Hale, T. Bell, J. Woodhouse. Middle row: J. Stoker, W. Carrol, G. Javis. Front row: J. Sample, T. Snowdon, W. Ormston, A. Turnbull, W. Sample.

Northern Amateur League, 1909

Includes: St Aidan's, Willington North End, Wallsend Slipway, Elm Villa

	P	W	L	D	Pts
Parkside	16	9	3	4	22
Windy Nook	15	9	3	3	21
Jarrow Caledonians	17	9	6	2	21
Shields Albion	18	7	5	6	20
Pelaw	18	7	6	5	19
Boldon Colliery	16	7	4	5	19
Willington St Aidan's	17	6	7	4	16
Wallsend Slipway	17	5	6	6	16
Felling ER	18	6	9	3	15
* Willington N. End	17	7	7	3	17
North Shields A	14	5	6	3	13
Wallsend Elm Villa	13	5	6	2	12
Adelaide A	18	3	10	5	11
New York United	16	3	10	3	9

(* Points deducted for playing an ineligible player)

Right: Willington North End, 1910. Extreme right, in the front row is Jack Renwick.

ROSEHILL ATHLETIC

Northern Amateur League   1934   Ground: unknown.

ROSEHILL HILLSIDE

Byker Amateur League   1909   Shields & District League   1911
Ground: Rosehill.

HOWDON STEAD MEMORIAL

North Shields Church League
Runners-up   1924-25
              1925-26
Wakefield Charity Cup
Winners 1924-25

Ground: Howdon Pit Heap.
Secretary: J.E. Ryan, 1920s.

Right: Howdon Stead, 1923.

SWANS FC

Northern Amateur League Division 2	Champions	1926-27
Northern Amateur League	Champions	1931-32, 1932-33
Northumberland Minor Cup	Winners	1934-35
Northumberland Amateur Cup	Winners	1934-35
Tyneside Amateur League	Champions	1957-58
Tyneside Amateur League Cup	Winners	1957-58
Wallsend Charity Cup	Runners-up	1957-58

Grounds: Swans Recreation, St Peter's Road.   Colours: Red and white.

Left: Swan Hunters, 1958-59. Back row: Carr, Hall, White, McKenzie, Cassidy, Shiel. Front row: Hope, Saddler, Lawes, Nutterly, Patterson.

HOOD HAGGIES FC

North Shields YMCA, League Runners up 1955-56
South East Northumberland League / Newcastle City Amateur League

Ground: Hood Haggies Sports.

Secretary: N. Heppell.

Right: Hood Haggies, 1965.
Back row:
J. High,
P. Graham,
R. Stacey,
P. Bailes,
T. Barkas,
J. Waterson.
Front row:
B. Robinson,
J. Pender,
H. Gibbons,
K. Graham,
S. McGhee.

WALLSEND ST PETER'S

Tynemouth YOC League,
Church of England   1912

Ground: Hospital Fields.   Manager: J. Athey, 1952.

Wallsend St Peter's, 1952. Back row: J. Athney, A. Ashbride, M. Clemitson, D. Heathcote, L. Alderson, H. Airlie, W. Holmers, G. Booth. Front row: B. Harrison, B. Lisle, J. Thornton, D. Kay, J. Kennedy.

COMMERCIAL PLASTICS

North Shields YMCA Cup   Runners-up 1955-56

Ground: Hood Haggies.

Right: Willington Commercial Plastics, 1955. Photo includes: Porter (goalkeeper), Swinhoe, Ward, Armstrong, Nichol, Taylor, Gent, Livingstone, Burns, Jackson, Briggs, Buck.

THOR TOOLS

North Shields YMCA   1960s   Newcastle & District   1990s

Ground: St Peter's Road.

Secretary / Manager: W. Stubbs, B. Richardson.

Left: Thor Tools FC, 1961. Includes: J. Duffy 2nd from left front row.

WALLSEND ST MICHAEL'S

Ground and league unknown, registered with Northumberland FA from 1949-52.

Secretary: J. Bradley.

SHELL MEX FC

Northern Amateur League Division 2   Champions 1937-38

Ground: Powder Monkey.

WALLSEND BRITISH LEGION

Northern Amateur League Cup   Winners   1911-12
South East Northumberland League   Cup Winners   1948-49
Northern Combination League   1947

Ground: unknown.   Secretary: J. Braven, 1949.

Northern Combination League, 1947-48

	P	W	L	D	F	A	Pts
Throckley W	17	13	1	3	59	22	27
Annfield Plain	16	8	3	5	57	28	21
Kingsway SC	17	7	5	5	60	30	19
Wardley W	16	9	6	1	55	32	19
Washington W	12	8	2	2	36	19	13
Barrington U	13	8	5	0	40	37	16
Huwoods SC	11	6	2	3	51	22	15
Crookhall CW	11	6	3	2	32	20	14
Usworth Col	13	6	5	2	24	22	14
N Fenham W	9	3	3	3	27	24	9
Reyrolies	13	4	8	1	29	45	9
Jarrow	14	3	10	1	16	60	7
LNER	9	1	6	2	16	49	4
Bentinck Cel	14	1	13	0	19	56	2
Wallsend BL	13	0	11	2	17	77	2

HOWDON BRITISH LEGION

Wallsend Charity Shield   Winners   1924-25, 1925-26
Tynemouth Dispensary Cup   Winners   1924-25, 1925-26
Northern Amateur League   Champions   1924-25, 1925-26
Northern Amateur League Cup   Winners   1926-27, 1927-28
Northumberland FA Amateur   Cup Winners   1922-3, 1924-5, 1925-6, 1926-27, 1928-29
Ingham Infirmary Cup   Winners   1929-30, 1930-31
Willington Quay Nursing Cup   Winners   1929-30, 1930-31

Ground: Howdon Pit Heap.

The Legion was one of the most successful teams the town has produced. They also ran a second team in the Newcastle & District Welfare League.

Men who played for league clubs:

S. Henderson – Chelsea
W.B. Foster – Newcastle United

Right: Howdon British Legion players and officials with Ingham Infirmary Cup and Willington Quay Nursing Cup, 1929-30.

WALLSEND BOYS' CLUB (SENIORS)

Tynemouth & District League   Runners-up   1947-48
Wallsend & District League   1962-63
Newcastle Dispensary Cup   Runners-up   1961-62
Northern Alliance League Division 1   Present

Ground: Bigges Main.   Colours: Green and yellow.
Secretary: P. Kirkley.   Managers: V. Carick, A. Gibson, S. Cuggy.

The Boys' Club has just restarted a senior team after many years but are more famous for the number of players they produce from their very successful junior set up – 62 at the last count as featured on pages 23-25. This list doesn't include at least four times that number of players that have played reserve team football and served apprenticeships with professional league clubs without quite making the grade.

   Wallsend Boys' Club down the years has always had great management teams with the likes of Peter Kirkley, John McNally, Steve Dale, Kevin Bell, Sid Sharpe, Terry Sweeney, Alan Jarvis and many more too numerous to mention giving up their time and expertise to make sure the football club has been and continues to be a great success.

Left: Wallsend Boys' Club, 1950.
Back row: T. Fairbridge, T. Potts, J. Breckon, W. Young, B. Laws, M. Murphy, R. Oliver.
Front row: W. Howarth, D. Gibbins, E. Ashcroft, V. Donnelly, L. Scullion, K. Flannery.

Wallsend & District League, October 1962

	P	W	D	L	F	A	Pts
Bigges Main	7	4	1	2	31	24	9
Walker Ath	5	4	0	1	24	19	8
Neptune Ath	7	4	0	3	51	22	8
Wallsend BC	5	4	0	1	26	13	8
Walls'd Pk V	6	4	0	2	25	16	8
Wallsend St Col	4	3	0	1	17	7	6
Rising Sun	5	3	0	2	15	15	6
Wallsend Celt	4	1	1	2	8	14	3
Wallsend YC	6	1	1	4	11	22	3
Walker Celtic	4	1	0	3	3	13	2
Royal Engin'rs	7	0	1	6	6	48	1
Wallsend Ams	2	0	0	2	3	17	0

WALLSEND ATHLETIC

Gosforth Amateur League		1909-10
Northern Amateur League		1910-11
South East Northumberland League	Cup Winners	1960-61
Tyneside Amateur League	Champions	1963-64, 1964-65, 1965-66
Northern Alliance	Runners-up	1968-69
Newcastle Dispensary Cup	Winners	1969-70
Northern Alliance Challenge Cup	Runners-up	1970-71
Wallsend Charity Cup	Winners	1974-75, 1963-64
Wallsend Charity Cup	Runners-up	1959-60
South East Hospital Cup		1967-68

Ground: St Peter's Road, Wallsend Rec, Churchill Playing Field.
Managers: C. Marr, B. Canfield.   Club colours: Blue and white stripes, blue shorts.

There was a Wallsend Athletic playing in 1910 in the Northern Amateur League, but Athletic re-started life in 1956 when most of the West End team moved to play under the management of Cyril Marr and Bob Canfield. They played in the South East Northumberland League and lifted the cup in the 1960-61 season before moving to the Tyneside Amateur League where they enjoyed a lot of success. They joined the Alliance in 1970 but began to go into decline when Bob Canfield and Brian Flynn left to run the newly formed Lindisfarne team. Although still managed by Cyril Marr, the club began to struggle and rejoined the Tyneside Amateur League and eventually folded around 1990.

Above: Wallsend Athletic, 1963. Back row: H. Wilkinson, E. Mann, D. O'Field, L. McDonald, F. Stephenson, M. Gibbons. Front row: K. Robson, A. Gallon, G. Wright, J. Warne, A. Smith.

Left: Wallsend Athletic, 1958. Back row: Tunmore, Rogerson, Cileno, Timney, McDonald, Groundsel. Front row: Brunskill, Gilmore, Scott, Thornton, L. Turnbull.

Newspaper Report – Newcastle Dispensary Cup Final, 1969-70
Large Crowd at Final

A better balanced Wallsend Athletic side defeated Wallsend Celtic in the final of the Newcastle Dispensary Cup on Friday. Athletic won 3-0 in a very good match watched by a large crowd. Montgomery scored two for Athletic and earned the commemorative statuettes given to both winners and runners-up alike.

Wallsend Athletic, 1964-65. Back row: C. Marr (Secretary), G. Warne (Committee), ?, D. Parkin, ?, E. Mann, P. O'Donnell, E. Stephenson, B. Flynn (Committee), B. Canfield (Manager). Front row: J. Humphreys (Committee), ?, ?, G. Wright, G. Hordon, ?, ?.

Tyneside Amateur League – final table, 1980-81

	P	W	D	L	F	A	Pts
Heddon Institute	26	18	5	3	75	32	41
Innisfree SC	26	17	6	3	69	27	40
Marden Athletic	26	16	7	3	67	29	39
Percy Main Athletic	26	16	6	4	65	34	38
D.H.S.S.	26	17	1	8	79	39	35
Wallsend Athletic	26	14	4	8	59	44	32
Proctor & Gamble	26	11	7	8	52	37	29
Gateshead Park Rangers	26	10	3	13	42	50	23
Walkergate CC	26	9	3	14	40	47	21
Michell Bearings	26	10	1	15	51	65	21
Winlaton	26	8	3	15	56	66	19
Victor Products	26	7	2	17	40	77	16
Byker CA	26	1	3	22	32	98	5
Benfield BC	26	2	1	23	29	111	5

Left: Wallsend Athletic, 1965. Back row: J. Brecken, D. Parkin, E. Mann, D. Bianchi, P. O'Donnell, F. Stevenson. Front row: A. Winskill, A. Gallon, M. Gibbons, J. Warne, B. Whitfield.

WALLSEND CORINTHIANS

South East Northumberland League	Champions	1954-55, 1955-56, 1957-58, 1959-60, 1960-61
Northern Combination		1963
South East Northumberland League Cup	Winners	1955-56, 1956-57, 1957-58
Wallsend Charity Cup	Winners	1952-53, 1957-58, 1958-59, 1961-62, 1969-70
Newcastle Dispensary Cup	Winners	1960-61
Northumberland Minor Cup	Runners-up	1958-59
Northumberland Junior Cup	Winners	1960-61, 1962-63
Northumberland Miners Welfare League Cup	Winners	1969-70
Northumberland Aged Miners Cup	Runners-up	1969-70

Ground: Heaton Terrace, 1950s. Bigges Main, 1960s. St Peter's Road, 1970s.
Club colours: White shirts, black shorts.   Secretary: J. Wood, 1945.

Always a very good side with the likes of the Flannery brothers and Jimmy McDonald playing season after season, Corinthians dominated the South East Northumberland League in the 1950s and early '60s before moving briefly into the Northern Combination where they finished fourth in the 1963-64 season before folding.

Corinthians also ran a very successful junior side which lifted the Northumberland Junior Cup twice. After appearing to fold in 1964, the Corinthians joined the Northumberland Miners' Welfare League in the 1969-70 season with a very strong squad managed by Billy Todd and playing at St Peter's Road. They lifted the League KO Cup in their first season along with the Wallsend Charity Cup but only lasted a couple of seasons before finishing.

A Wallsend Corinthians re-appeared in the Tyneside Amateur League in the mid-1970s under totally different management but folded for good around 1980.

Corinthians, 1969-70. Mr R. Wilson presenting the Wallsend Charity Cup to the Corinthians at their presentation night. Included: J. O'Donnell, J. Atkinson, D. Cullen, J. Reynolds, J. Rice, W. Dodds, E. Breeze, W. Small, J. Storey, W. Young, R. Young, B. Todd.

Corinthians players with Wallsend Charity Cup, 1955.

South East Northumberland League – Final table, 1956-57

	P	W	D	L	F	A	Pts
Corinthians	26	32	8	3	112	35	46
Cullercoats	26	22	1	3	98	31	45
Victor Wel	26	16	0	10	69	48	32
Forest Hall	26	14	3	9	81	62	31
YMCA Ath	26	12	5	9	65	46	29
Burrad'n W	24	12	4	8	77	38	28
W'd WERA	25	13	2	10	70	55	28
Square V	26	10	3	13	57	70	23
Whitley A	25	10	3	12	68	88	23
Swans Wel	26	8	2	16	75	99	18
Backworth	26	7	2	17	63	82	16

Left: Corinthians Jnrs, 1959. Back row: S. Hitchins (manager), J. Kirtley, D. Winskill, E. Stephenson, D. Bartram, G. Little, N. Dunn. Front row: J. McCrae, M. Cuskern, G. Parkin, D. Burns, P. Flaherty, F. Coulter (trainer).

NEERC

North Eastern Amateur League   Cup Winners 1962-3
Newcastle & District Welfare League   1960s
Tyneside Amateur League Subsidiary Cup   Winners   1983-4
Northern Alliance Amateurs Cup   Winners   1988-9
Northern Combination

Ground: Kings Road South.
Club colours: Light blue.
Secretary: J. Brennan.

NEERC ran two teams at their beautifully kept sports ground at Kings Road South, but finished as a Wallsend-based club when the ground was sold for building in the late 1990s.

Right: NEERC, 1970.

McEwans Northern Alliance First Division – final table, 1989-90							
	P	W	D	L	F	A	Pts
Westerhope	30	22	7	1	87	23	73
Walker	30	19	4	7	93	47	62
Hexham	30	18	7	5	62	35	61
Carlisle City	30	18	4	8	89	44	58
Blyth KB	30	17	7	6	93	52	58
Ryton	30	16	7	7	66	37	55
Stobswood	30	15	2	13	55	58	47
N. Counties	30	13	5	12	71	57	44
NEERC	30	13	4	13	67	59	43
Winlaton	30	12	4	14	52	62	40
New York	30	9	3	18	59	65	30
Wallsend RS	30	9	3	18	38	83	30
University	30	8	4	18	42	66	28
Heddon	30	8	4	18	45	86	19
Bohemians	30	5	2	23	37	93	17
Pegswood	30	2	5	23	26	114	10

WALLSEND FC

Tyneside Amateur League Cup	Winners	1967-68, 1968-69
Northern Combination Challenge Cup	Runners-up	1967-68
Tyneside Amateur League	Runners-up	1969-70
Northumberland Amateur Cup	Winners	1968-69
Wallsend Charity Cup		1965-66, 1966-7, 1968-9

Ground: Bigges Main.
Secretary: A. Deagle.

Chairman: E. Brown.
Colours: Green shirts, gold shorts.

Wallsend FC first appeared in the Northern Combination as a replacement for Corinthians, they also had some of the same management team! Wallsend also ran a second team in the Tyneside Amateur League.

Right: Wallsend FC, 1968. Back row: K. Fletcher, W. Fleming, W. Waddell, S. Craig, G. Little, M. Fairley, B. Oakley. Front row: P. Boyle, I. Watts, D. Redhead, R. Anderson, R. Winskill.

Northern Combination – final table, 1967-68

	P	W	D	L	F	A	Pts
West Wylam & Prudhoe	30	22	4	4	86	41	48
Blue Star Welfare	30	20	6	4	87	44	46
Swalwell FC	30	19	6	5	91	53	44
Newburn	30	19	3	8	73	47	41
Whitley Bay Reserves	30	17	4	9	82	51	38
Wallsend	30	14	9	7	66	41	37
Whickham	30	13	8	9	73	63	34
Blyth Spartan Reserves	30	14	4	12	61	53	32
Winlaton West End	30	13	2	15	65	71	28
North Shields Reserves	30	9	5	16	54	63	23
Gosforth & Coxlodge Wel	30	9	5	16	50	76	23
Parson's Athletics	30	8	6	16	57	71	22
Heaton Stannington	30	10	2	18	56	77	22
Shankhouse	30	6	6	18	58	79	18
Angus United	30	4	6	20	43	112	14
Ministry of Social Security	30	3	4	23	34	96	10

MONITOR ENGINEERING FC

Newcastle & District League, Division 2   Runners-up 1971-72

Ground: St Peter's Road.

WALLSEND TOWN

Wearside League		1973-81
Wearside League	Champions	1978-9
Northern Alliance		1981-6
Northumberland Senor Bowl	Runners-up	1984

Ground: Wallsend Sports Centre.
Managers: R. Bell, R. Cook, J. Watson, P. Flaherty, T. Cassidy.
Secretary: B. Lisle.
Chairman: A. Bloomfield.
Colours: Green shirts, gold shorts.

Wallsend Town FC started up in the 1973-74 season when they joined the Wearside League under manager Billy Bell and quickly became one of the strongest sides in the area. Unfortunately they couldn't sustain their early success and after changing homes more than once in an effort to attract more support folded in the late 1980s.

Wallsend Town reformed under a different management in the 1998-99 season and rejoined the Wearside League Division 2. They also ran a team in the Tyneside Amateur League and will now appear in the Durham Alliance League for the 2014-15 season.

Wallsend Town, 1974-75. Back row: J. Downey, R. Cook, W. Lisgo, K. Wilson, T. O'Connor, V. Hillier. Front row: R. Percy, C. Arthur, J. Montgomery, P. Cunningham, H. Trotter.

Wearside League		1998
Northern Alliance		2001
Northern Alliance Challenge Cup	Winners	2000-01
Northumberland Benevolent Bowl	Winners	2006-07

Ground: Langdale Centre.

Secretary: D. Grandini.

Billy Bell, Wallsend Town manager, 1974-75.

Wearside League – final table, 1979				
	P	W	D	Pts
Wallsend	32	21	5	47
Wingate	32	21	4	46
Whickham	32	17	10	44
Boldon CA	32	18	7	43
South Shields	32	16	11	43
Hartlepool Res	32	15	5	37
Chester-le-Street	32	13	10	36
Blue Star	32	19	5	35
Annfield Plain	32	13	6	32
Easington CW	32	11	8	30
Ryhope CW	32	8	11	27
Eppleton CW	32	8	6	22
Washington	32	7	8	20
Reyrolles	32	8	4	20
Roker	32	5	8	18
Heaton Stan	32	6	5	17
Murton	32	4	9	17

Wallsend Town reached the last eight of the FA Vase in the 1974-75 season before losing to Lincoln United:

Round 1: Annan Athletic

Round 2: Heaton Stannington

Round 2: Eppleton

Round 4: Sheffield

Round 5: Lincoln United

Newspaper Report – Wallsend Wearside Wonders, 1979

Wallsend Town are the champions of the Wearside League for the first time in their five year history. And they clinched the title in the best possible way by hitting strugglers Murton for six in their final match of the season, in front of their own fans at the Rising Sun. It was too much for rivals Wingate who were going down 2-0 at Blue Star, leaving Wallsend a point clear at the top of the table. A win at Blue Star would have given Town's Durham rivals the Wearside Championship. It had been a superb second half of the season performance by Wallsend. It looked as if the winter was going to hit the snow bound Rising Sun team in a big way as the fixtures piled up in the New Year. But the team, with all the squad playing its part, has come through with some brilliant goal-scoring displays. The Wallsend lads have found the net an incredible 88 times this season in just 32 games a scoring rate of almost three goals a game leaving them joint Wearside League top-scorers with last year's FA Vase Wembley heroes, Blue Star. The defence has also played its part in Town's big success, and only two sides have conceded less goals then the Rising Sun outfit. It has been a great first season as manager for new boss John Watson, who only took over at the Rising Sun midway through the season after Peter Flaherty left to join Northern League Blyth Spartans. But Flaherty deserves stacks of credit too. Through hard work and dedication he built the team up and paved the way for the last week's championship glory, which followed just a handful of months after he left the club.

Peter Flaherty.

VICTOR PRODUCTS FC

Tynemouth & District League	1959
Tyneside Amateur League	1970s-1980s

Ground: St Peter's Road.

Colours: Blue and white stripes.

Secretary: K. Hutchinson, 1956

Right: Victor Products, 1967. Back row: D. Rowley, D. Stoller, M. Howey, D. Roberts, M. Hogg, T. Spencer. Front row: A. Weavers, K. Grainger, V. Wood, P. Usher, J. Egan, J. Nichol.

WALLSEND TRADESMEN

Newcastle & District Business House Wednesday League	1959
Northumberland FA Mid-week Challenge Cup Winners	1930-31, 1931-32, 1933-34

Ground: North Road.

WALLSEND COMPANIONS FC

Newcastle & District Welfare League   1989
Ground: Battle Hill.   Secretary: J. Walton, J. Fisher.   Colours: All green.

Newcastle & District League Division One, 1988-89, final placings

	P	W	D	L	F	A	Pts
Hazelrigg CW	28	20	6	2	82	36	46
Shieldfield Globe	28	21	3	4	94	41	45
Newcastle Telegraph	28	18	3	7	87	60	39
Blaydon Huntsman	28	16	5	7	95	56	37
Duke of Cumberland	28	14	7	7	67	48	35
Scotswood Alliance	28	14	4	10	80	76	32
Wylam FC	28	14	3	11	67	48	31
Ouseburn CC	28	12	2	14	68	73	26
Bridon Fibres	28	10	4	14	65	69	24
Walker FOS	28	9	5	14	57	84	23
Seaton Burn SC	28	7	5	16	48	76	19
Benwell Mitre	28	9	1	18	51	85	19
Coxlodge Welfare	28	6	6	16	46	67	18
Wallsend Comp	28	6	3	19	45	90	15
Percy Arms	28	3	5	20	42	85	11

COOKSONS FC

Northern Amateur League
Northern Amateur League Division 2   Champions   1927-28
Northern Amateur League Challenge Cup   Winners   1927-28
South East Northumberland League   1980s
Newcastle & District Welfare League   1948

Ground: St Peter's Road.

Manager: P. Bagnall, 1945.
P. Hathaway, 1980s.

Left: Cooksons in the 1980s with Purvis Hathaway (manager).

Right: Cookson FC, 1920. Back row: Mr Chambers, C. Foster, Salmon, Short, Edger, Wilson, Fletcher, Stammers. Front row: Roxburgh, Sayers, J. Webster, Bullock, W. Webster.

CARVILLE FC

Newcastle City Amateur League 1984   Ground: unknown.

PARMETRADA FC

League and ground: unknown.   Secretary: H. Hardisty.

Appeared in the Northumberland FA handbook for one season only 1950-51.

WILLINGTON QUAY SAINTS

South East Northumberland League Cup	Winners	2001-02
Tyneside Amateur League Division 2	Winners	2002-03
Northumberland Minor Cup	Runners-up	2006-07
Northern Alliance	Present	

Ground: Rising Sun.   Colours: Blue and yellow.
Chairman: T. Ford.   Secretary: T. Allan.
Manager: L. Coulter.

Willington Quality Saints are one of our six Saturday teams still competing and are currently in the Northern Alliance 2nd Division.

Willington Quay Saints FC. Back row: W. Fidler, G. Doherty, S. Cape, G. Lowes, A. McBeth, S. Partridge, S. Telefoni, S. Duffield. Middle row: S. Ferrier, J. Allan, L. Best, G. Pugh, M. Austin, D. Hutchinson, A. Duffield, C. Henderson, S. King, D. Johnston, G. Johnston, I. McCartney, A. Davison (com), K. Chirnside. Front row: L. Taylor, N. Clynch, L. Coulter (coach), P. Donkin (manager), T. Ford (ass man), M. Henderson, K. Burip, M. Turner.

HIGH HOWDON SC

Tyneside Amateur League   Northern Alliance 2014-15

Ground: St Peter's Road.   Colours: Blue   Secretary: R. Dunn.

High Howdon SC is another of our Saturday teams playing in the Northern Alliance Division 2.

WALLSEND ST LUKE'S

Wallsend & District League		1910
Northern Amateur League Division 2	Champions	1930-31
Northumberland Minor Cup	Winners	1939-40
Northern Combination	Runners-up	1941-42
North Eastern Amateur League Division 2	Champions	1947-48, 1953-54
North Eastern Amateur League	Champions	1954-55
Wallsend Charity Cup	Winners	1953-54, 1954-55
Northern Amateur League Cup	Winners	1955-56
Newcastle Dispensary Cup	Winners	1953-54, 1955-56, 1956-57, 1957-58

Ground: North Road.
Managers: P. Middlemas, F. Herdman.
Colours: Blue, white shorts.

A well supported team, St Luke's ran two sides with the reserves competing in the North Eastern Amateur League. When one of their long serving management team Percy Middlemast retired in 1961, two thousand people turned up for his testimonial game between an 'old stars' and Wallsend select teams. A programme with the number 1503 shows two strong sides that played out a 5-5 draw.

St Luke's folded in the mid-1960s when the North Road Ground was used for the building of the Lindisfarne Club.

Wallsend St Luke's, 1954, reserves and officials. Includes players, back row: H. Tilyer, Wilson, Redhead, Anderson, Charlton, Thompson, Dobson, Orr, Swan, Fairley, Stephenson, Alison, Brotherston, Maynes, Tubman. Middle row: Hundrey, Lawson, Dixon, Rennison, Cartwright, McKenna. Front row: Gillie, Thompson, Aitken, Jackson.

Wallsend St Luke's Reserves, on tour in Jersey in 1958.

Wallsend Charity Cup Final, 1955. St Luke's v Rising Sun. Robson, the St Luke's centre half, plays the ball back to keeper Tubman – challenged by Howe and Brownlee.

Players who went on to play league football:

Bell – Derby County, 1939
Maxwell – South Shields
G. McGill – Cardiff City, 1920
E. Gibson – Aston Villa, 1920
C. Crowe – Newcastle United, 1949
J. Hedley – Sunderland, 1948
Bill McKinney – Newcastle, 1950s

Right: St Luke's v West Allotment. Tubman saves against West Allotment in a Northern Amateur Cup tie in 1955. St Luke's went on to win 4-2.

St Luke's, 1957. Back row: H. Curry (secretary), Fairley, Peake, Hodgson, Young, Howling, Poolan, Hodgson. Front row: McKinnon, Foster, Allen, Hudson, Patton.

A cartoon of Vincent Redhead, St Luke's, 1954.

The Percy Middlemast Testimonal Match

Good Friday, KO 11 am, 31st March, 1961 at the North Road Ground, Wallsend

Old Stars Versus Wallsend select

Ferguson's XI: John Mapson (ex-Sunderland), Bill Rochford (ex-Portsmouth), Tom Callender (ex-Gateshead), Benny Craig (Newcastle United trainer), George Hardwick (ex-Middlesbrough and England Captain), Jimmy Woodburn (ex-Newcastle United), Charlie Crowe (ex-Newcastle United), Arthur Wright (Sunderland) George Curtis (Sunderland trainer), Len Shackleton (ex-Newcastle, Sunderland and England), Charlie Mitten (Newcastle United manager), Charlie Ferguson.

Wallsend Select: W. Young, C. Allinson, R. Mckay, E. Howling, M. Robson, L. Fairley, J. Miller, L. Hiftle, S. Jackson, B. Walker and J. Kiddie. Probable half-time changes: E. Chambers, N. Allen, V. Redhead, W. Dodds, P. Blagburn, K. Flannery, R. Chambers and R. Nichols.

Officials – Referee: T.P. Laverick. Linesmen: H. White, R.N. Newby.

Trainers – Jimmy Craggs and Jack Tubman.

Kick off by Stan Seymour, Newcastle United Director.

1 Penny Donation

RISING SUN

Northern Amateur League　　　　Northern Combination
Northern Alliance　　　　　　　　Miners' Welfare League

Northern Amateur League	Champions	1946-47, 1952-53, 1953-54, 1954-55
Northern Amateur League	Winners	1946-47, 1947-48, 1949-50, 1954-55
Northumberland Amateur Cup	Winners	1946-47, 1949-50, 1954-55
Northumberland Minor Cup	Winners	1972-73
Heddon Homes Cup	Winners	1949-50, 1950-51, 1954-55
Northern Alliance Cup	Runners-up	1989-90, 1958-59
Northumberland Junior Cup	Winners	1952-53, 1970-71, 1976-77
Wallsend Charity Cup	Winners	1956-57, 1945-46, 1946-7, 1950-51

Ground: Rising Sun Welfare.　　Colours: Red, white shorts.
Managers: E. Gustard, W. Wood, 1945.

One of Wallsend's strongest sides over the years, the 'Suns' halcyon days were in the 1940s and '50s when they had some outstanding players. The Sun also ran a strong team in the Miners' Welfare League and a very successful junior side.

Left: Rising Sun, 1954. Back row: B. Dodding, K. McKinney, B. McKay, W. Young, H. Gibson, Will Dodds. Front row: Wal Dodds, H. Brownlee, R. Hay, E. Howling, H. Knox.

Right: Rising Sun, 1967. Back row: D. Armstrong, J. Archer, G. Tubman, K. Dixon, B. Neal, J. Swann, K. Elliott, R. Thompson, A. Winskill. Front row: J. Berry, W. McMillan, R. McCulloch, I. Atkinson, T. Ovens.

Left: Rising Sun, 1968-69, with Miners' Welfare League Cup. Back row: R. Thompson, M. Marshall, D. Heywood, J. Tubman, C. Davis, J. Swann. Front row: B. McMillan, R. McCulloch, W. Tubman, W. Neale, G. Tubman, J. Scott.

Northern Amateur League, January 1948

	P	W	L	D	F	A	Pts
Percy Main	19	16	1	2	80	30	34
Rising Sun	19	13	2	4	64	28	30
W Allotment	18	10	5	3	66	46	23
Ringtons W	19	10	6	3	66	45	23
Clelands	16	9	4	3	60	36	21
Seaton Del	16	9	4	3	48	28	21
Bohemians	18	8	7	3	62	63	19
Heaton Stann	19	8	10	1	57	56	17
Seghill	16	8	7	1	44	42	17
N Sq Pres	16	7	8	1	49	55	15
Parson Ath	15	5	7	3	34	44	13
Kings College	15	5	9	1	43	40	11
Wallsend St L	15	4	9	2	34	55	10
Gosforth Par	17	3	12	2	37	72	8
Thermal	16	2	11	3	28	52	7
N Shields YM	18	1	16	1	33	110	3

Right: Rising Sun, 1957-58. Back row: Adams, Adamson, Beckwith, Tubman, Redhead, Anderson. Front row: Robinson, Brownlee, Brannen, Rawling, Knox.

Left: Rising Sun Reserves, 1957-58. Back row: Marshall, Dunleavey, Moore, O'Donnell, Scotford, Southwell. Front row: Bryhem, Cheetham, Elliott, Conway, Kennedy, McCarthy (mascot).

WALLSEND MINERS

Wallsend & District League Cup	Winners	1961
Wallsend & District League Cup	League Runners-up	1962-63

Ground: Rising Sun.　　　　　　　Manager: J. Hooks.

Independent of the Rising Sun teams, the side was made up of lads that worked at the pit or used the Miners' Welfare Club.

WALLSEND PARK VILLA

Wallsend & District League　　　　North Shields YMCA League 1964

Ground: Swans Rec.　　　　　　　Manager: H. Gibson.

Park Villa were resurrected again in the 1960s by Wallsend Football stalwart Harry Gibson. Although they didn't win any trophies they were always a well-run friendly club.

Left: Wallsend Park Villa Team, 1970. Includes: Captain H. Reed shaking H. Gibson's hand, P. Martin, B. Clarke, T. Strutt, J. Evans, T. Davison, J. Heward, J. Richardson, A. Dawson, J. Young, P. Mawson.

WALLSEND ST COLUMBA'S / ST COLUMBA'S CASUALS

South East Northumberland League	Newcastle City Amateur League
Wallsend & District League	1910
Wallsend Charity Cup	Winners 1962-63
Wallsend & District League Cup	Runners-up 1962-63
South East Northumberland League	Runners-up 1967-68
Percy Hedley Cup	Winners 1961

Ground: St Peter's Road.　　　　　Colours: Red, white shorts.
Managers: T. Morrison, T. Wylie, J. Tunmore.

The parish team goes back to the early days of Wallsend football, ran by Tommy Morrison and Tom Wylie in the 1950s and '60s. They produced a lot of good footballers like the Flannery brothers, Billy Wright, Malcolm Peel, Ray Rooney and Pat McGloughlan, but they folded in the early 1970s when the Lindisfarne Catholic Club was built and it became the hub of the parish sports events.

St Columba's centre forward Billy Wright, who later went on to star with Whitley Bay in the Northern League, was transferred from the Saints to Ashington AFC in 1962 for the princely sum of £10 and five footballs.

Left: St Columba's. Billy Wright (No 9) playing for Whitley Bay in the final of the Northumberland Senior Cup against North Shields in 1970 at St James' Park. Wright scored two goals in a 4-0 victory.

Right: Wallsend St Columba's, 1967. Back row: R. Elliott, P. Burns, D. Mooney, T. Davidson, J. Dewhurst, A. Devine, B. Mooney, Dave Mooney. Front row: A. Wheeler, A. Waddle, T. Nash, J. Jones, D. Spark.

Left: Wallsend St Columba's, 1960. Back row: T. Morrison, A. Thompson, R. Rooney, J. McGloughlan, J. McDonald, J. Brass, Mr McGloughlan, Mr McDonald, Front row: P. Doran, J. Summers, D. Robson, A. Devine, ?, J. Hemy.

Left: Wallsend St Columba's, 1963. Back row: B. Convery, P. McKenna, P. McGloughlan, B. Townsend, B. Clark, R. Rooney, H. McKenna. Front row: M. Cuggy, J. Close, A. Thompson, J. Conway, J. Mooney.

Wallsend St Columba's, 1968. Back row: B. Braddick, R. Rooney, D. Spark, A. Devine, T. Davidson, D. Mooney. Front row: A Thompson, A. Wheeler, B. Mooney, A. Fletcher, B. Pumfrey.

St Columba's Jnrs, 1959, with the Percy Hedley Cup at North Road Ground after a victory over Corinthians. Bob Mooney is lifted shoulder high by his teammates: Billy Wright, Malcolm Peel, P. McKenna, Alex Innes, John Mooney, Bob Percy, Brian Jameson, Eric Trainor, Dave Souter, Kev Riley.

Newcastle City Amateur League – final table, 1963-64

	P	W	D	L	F	A	Pts
Wills Imp	30	27	2	1	183	36	56
Parson Ath	30	23	3	4	138	60	49
Walls'd St Col	30	16	9	5	86	51	41
PO Telephones	30	18	2	10	115	78	38
Wallsend Celtic	30	18	1	11	143	90	37
West End OB	30	18	0	12	108	87	36
Dunlop	30	14	5	11	77	78	33
Dunston R	30	15	2	13	111	119	32
North Vale	30	12	5	13	116	81	29
Walbottle CA	30	11	7	12	83	85	29
Taylor SC	30	12	4	14	91	87	28
Leam Lane	30	15	2	13	83	68	22
Gasconians	30	5	3	22	56	141	13
Inland Revenue	30	5	3	22	53	147	13
Tyne U	30	3	2	25	44	155	8
Hood Haggie	30	2	2	26	50	159	6

WALLSEND CELTIC

Tyneside League	1896
Northern Amateur League	
Wallsend & District League	1962
Newcastle City Amateur League Subsidiary Cup	Winners 1967-68
South East Northumberland League	
Tyneside Amateur League	Champions 1972-73
Newcastle Dispensary Cup	Runners-up 1969-70
Northumberland Minor Cup	Winners 1932-33
Newcastle Dispensary Cup	Winners 1970-71
Northumberland Minor Cup	Runners-up 1970-71
Northumberland Amateur Cup	Runners-up 1970-71
Wallsend Charity Cup	Winners 1971-72
South East Northumberland Hospital Cup	Winners 1973-74

Ground: St Peter's Road.
Colours: Green and white hoops.

Managers: J. Powers, J. Justice.

At the turn of the twentieth century, Celtic were competing with the top local sides and regularly competed in the Northumberland Senior Cup.

A strong club in the 1930s, Celtic were reformed again in the early 1960s by Joe Powers and Joe Justice and with good players like Peter Baker, Banty Neal and Kenny Farley and had a very successful team before folding in the late 1970s.

Wallsend Celtic, 1920.

Newspaper Report

Northumberland Senior Cup
2nd Round 1896

Willington Athletic 3
Wallsend Celtic 1

At Willington, before a tremendous gate. Athletics had the best of the play all through and in the first half Jones and Lamb scored, whilst Simpson got one for the visitors. After the interval Porter scored. For some time play was very even, each side in turn being aggressive. No further score was added and the game ended:
Willington 3 Celtic 1

Wallsend Celtic. Back row: T. Strutt, A. Henderson, C. Irvine, P. Baker, J. Dewhurst, F. Brennan, F. Buck, B. Strutt, B. Neal, J. Justice. Front row: D. Elliott, B. Smith, K. Farley, M. Cuggy, J. Powers.

Newspaper Report – Cup Triumphs for Celtic, 1971-72

Wallsend Celtic brought off a magnificent cup double to finish the season and make up to some extent for disappointments in two other cups and the Tyneside Amateur League. After being beaten finalists in the Northumberland County Amateur and Minor Cups and finishing third in their first season in the Tyneside Amateur League, Celtic showed admirable grit to beat Percy Main 4-2 in the final of the South-East Northumberland Hospitals Cup and then defeat local rivals Wallsend Athletic 1-0 to win Wallsend Charity Cup. Against Percy Main, Celtic were on top form, especially the defence. Celtic dictated play throughout the first half and R. Elliott opened the scoring when he tore through the main defence to crack a tremendous shot, which Beasley could only palm straight to Powers who scored. R. Elliott turned the main defence inside out with two goals to give Celtic a 3-1 lead, one goal from the penalty spot, Roseburgh scoring the Percy Main goal. Percy Main pulled back to 3-2 in the second half, but R. Elliott notched his hat trick to make the score 4-2. Against Wallsend Athletic, it was all Celtic, but the score was 0-0 at half time, despite some brilliant attacking football from the Celtic forwards. The only goal of the game came after five minutes of the second half when the ball ran loose to Powers from a goalmouth scramble who rammed the ball home to give Celtic their second trophy in four days.

Tyneside Amateur League, 1972-73

	P	W	D	F	A	Pts
Wallsend Cel	28	23	2	129	33	48
Ponteland U	28	21	3	109	38	45
Heaton Arg'e	28	19	3	97	41	41
Innisfree SC	28	18	2	111	56	38
St Nich Hosp	28	14	4	65	72	32
Walk'gate CC	28	13	4	66	70	30
Byker CC	28	11	6	58	71	28
Elm United	28	11	3	62	85	25
Heddon Inst	28	10	4	64	72	24
Vickers SC	28	9	6	62	71	24
DHSS Res	28	8	7	45	67	23
Ingersoll R'nd	28	7	8	63	88	22
Victor Prod	28	5	8	37	78	18
Proct/Gamble	28	4	6	59	99	14
Marden Ath	28	3	2	39	125	8

Above: Amateur Cup Final, 1972.

Left: Wallsend Celtic, 1969-70. Back row: Henderson, B. Strutt, C. Oliver, J. Miller, D. Elliott, P. Baker, B. Elliott. Front row: K. Farley, B. Smith, J. Powers, M. Cuggy, R. Elliott, R. Mann (mascot).

WALLSEND GORDON

Northern Amateur League Cup	Winners	1933-34
Northumberland Amateur Cup	Winners	1937-38
Tyneside Amateur League	Champions	1967-68
Northumberland Aged Miners Cup	Winners	1967-68
Newcastle Dispensary Cup	Winners	1967-68

Grounds: Western Field, St Peter's Road, Point Pleasant.
Colours: Blue, white shorts.
Managers: John Todd, 1930s. Billy Todd, 1960s.

A very successful team in the 1930s with players drawn mainly from the Gordon Square tenament block. The club was restarted by Billy Todd in the 1960s and turned out some very good sides until it folded for good in 1969.

Right: Wallsend Gordon, 1967. Back row: Davison, Mullen, Bianchi, Taylor, Bruce, Dodds. Front row: White, Oliver, Berry, Short, Rickman, Dowling.

WALLSEND CO-OP

Newcastle Business Houses Wednesday League
1940s – 1970s

Ground: North Road.

Left: Wallsend Co-op. Back row: J. Montgomery, ?, M. Oldfield, A. Parks, ?, L. Hope, J. Maughan. Front row: ?, B. Watson, ?, K. Beech, ?, ?.

SUNHOLME AMATEURS

League and ground unknown.   Secretary: W. Murray.

Appeared in the NFA Handbook for one season only, 1950-51.

CARVILLE POWER STATION FC

League and ground unknown.   Secretary: R. Teasdale.

Appeared in the FA Handbook for the 1951-52 season only.

CLELANDS FC

Northern Amateur League   1940s and 1950s

Ground: unknown.   Secretary: A. Marshall, 1945.

BIGGES MAIN FC

Wallsend & District League	Champions	1912-13
Wallsend & District League Cup	Winners	1912-13
Northern Amateur League	Champions	1934-35, 1935-36
Northern Amateur League Division 2	Champions	1925-26
Northern Amateur League Challenge Cup	Winners	1931-32, 1934-35, 1936-37
Northumberland FA Amateur Cup	Winners	1933-34

Grounds: Bigges Main where the golf driving range now is. Powder Monkey, 1940s-50s.
Secretaries: W.A. Robson, 1930s. R. Vinisoms, 1950.

The Bigges Main village team were a very good side in the 1920s and '30s but their demise came with the demolition of the hamlet in the mid-1930s. Although started up again in the late 1940s and again in the '60s they didn't last long and finished for good after a short spell in the Wallsend & District League.

Players who when on to play league football:

Sam Cuggy – Hull City
Frank Cuggy – Sunderland & England
Albert Stubbins – Liverpool & England

Right: Bigges Main FC, 1904-05. Holding the ball is Sam Cuggy of Hull City fame. On his immediate left is his brother Frank who went on to play for Sunderland and England.

Bigges Main, 1954. Back row: E. Hislop, P. Pearce, L. Duncan, J. McTigue, A. Errington, L. Elliott. Front row: B. Campbell, A. Coxon, L. Scullion, B. Corkhill, D. McFarlane.

Right: Bigges Main v De-La-Rue, 1954. Duncan, the Bigges Main keeper, saves from De-La-Rue forward as full back Pearce covers.

WILLINGTON ROYAL BRITISH LEGION

Newcastle City Amateur League Cup   Winners   1974-75
Newcastle City Amateur League   Champions   1974-75
Tyneside Amateur League   1970s

Ground: St Peter's Road.   Colours: Yellow, black shorts.

Secretary: J. High.

Left: Willington British Legion FC, 1975, with the Newcastle City Amateur League and Cup trophys. Back row: T. Thompson, C. Ward, R. Dowdell, J. Flynn, M. Scott, P. Smith, J. High, J. Nichol. Front row: J. Dowdell, L. Jamieson, D. Boyle, I. Rickalton, D. Rycroft.

SWINBURNE UNITED

North Shields YMCA
League, 1959

Ground: Swans Rec.

Right: Swinburne United, 1959. Back row: J. Harkins, G. Yeoman, A. High, H. KcKenna, R. Waddle, J. Joyce. Front row: K. Gray, R. Heron, B. Aitken, J. McGhee, D. Parker.

SWANS UNITED

Newcastle & District Welfare League   Runners-up   1964-65
Newcastle City Amateur League   Subsidiary Cup Winners 1970

Formed: 1959.   Ground: Swans Rec.   Manager: J. Tunmore.

Swans United celebrating victory in 1970. The mascot is seven-year-old John Tunmore, son of the team's manager.

Above: Swans United striker Joe Thewlis heads goalwards in the League Cup victory over Vickers Armstrong in 1971.

*Right: Swans United, 1976.
Back row: G. Smith, B. McIver, R. Dowdell, V. Mulroy, J. Dowdell, P. Smitch, T. McGlosson, J. Tunmore.
Front row: H. Gibson, B. Oliver, J. Blakey, H. Armstrong, T. O'Gara, G. Richardson.*

*Left: Swans United, 1971
Back row:
J. Hall,
T. O'Gara,
J. Dowdell,
T. McGloggan,
T. McGhee,
A. Smith,
T. Hannard.
Front row:
J. Blakey,
A. Reay,
J. Thewlis,
R. Dowdell,
V. Mulroy,
S. Turner
(mascot).*

WALLSEND THERMAL FC

Northern Amateur League 1930s
Newcastle & District Welfare League

Ground: Thermal Sports Ground, now the golf club.
Secretary: J. Hiftle, 1930s. A. Chambers, 1945. Colours: Red, white shorts.

M.H. Tapken left to join Newcastle United and played in the first team in 1933. Going on to make 122 appearances before being transferred to Manchester United.

Right: Wallsend Thermal, 1964. Includes: J. Grievson, Joe Powers, B. Watson, B. Rushton, Joe Justice.

WALLSEND WEST END

Byker Amateur League		1909
Shields & District League	Champions	1910-11
Shields & District League KO Bowl	Winners	1910-11
Northern Amateur League		1930s
Newcastle City Amateur League		1950s
Newcastle Dispensary Cup	Winners	1961-62
Wallsend Charity Cup	Runners-up	1956-57

Ground: St Peter's Road, 1950s. Colours: White shirts, black shorts.
Secretary: Alf Senior, 1930s. West End folded in the mid-1960s.

Newcastle City Amateur League, final table, 1962-63

	P	W	D	L	F	A	Pts
Dunlop	30	26	3	1	144	28	55
Parsons	30	21	1	8	156	72	43
Wills Imperial	30	19	3	8	108	60	41
PO Telephones	30	17	3	10	100	64	37
St Mary's	30	17	2	11	88	54	36
North Vale	30	15	5	10	77	59	35
Wallsend WERA	30	16	2	12	69	62	34
Fenham WE	30	13	6	11	101	80	32
Dunston Rovers	30	15	1	14	84	104	31
Angus United	30	13	2	15	79	93	28
Taylors SC	30	12	2	16	78	96	26
West End OB	30	12	1	17	85	97	25
Gasconians	30	11	3	16	72	111	25
Ryl Marines VR	30	5	3	22	51	131	13
Walbottle Am	30	4	4	22	37	129	12
Tyne United	30	3	1	26	47	133	7

WERA – Winners of the Newcastle Dispensary Cup, 1962. Left to right: B. Crawford, G. Cross, R. Moore, J. Sanderson, D. Birdsey, C. Devine, T. Howard, C. Thompson (goalkeeper), M. Ovington, R. Duffell, Mr T. Fenwick, MD of Fenwicks. presented the cup to captain L. Debbage.

Newspaper Report – Cup Win, But WERA Leave it Late

More than 500 spectators saw the final of the Newcastle Dispensary Cup fought out between two Wallsend clubs, WERA and Boys' Club on Easter Monday morning at the Newcastle United ground at North Road, Wallsend … In the bright sunshine Boys' Club did all the early attacking but many good chances were lost. The WERA defence was sound and their opponents had to resort to long shots … After half a hour of continual defence, WERA broke through but Graham at once deprived Cross of possession. It was not until the 36th minute that WERA got the ball over the Boys' Club line, a corner yielded by Emmerson, but this was immediately cleared … In the last five minutes of the half, Boys' Club did everything except score. After the interval it was WERA's turn to attack … With only 90 seconds left for play left back Moore sent in a rising shot to Britt's right. Britt could do no more than deflect the ball into the corner of the net. The jubilant West End surged back straight from the centre, and Duffell tricked the defence and shot past Britt to clinch the issue with a brilliant goal. Mr Trevor Fenwick of Newcastle donor of the trophy, presented it to the winners. Mr W.F. Atkinson vice chairman of the cup competition thanked Newcastle United for the use of the ground. He was especially grateful to the Wallsend News for the excellent publicity given to the final. Mr J.L. Taylor, secretary said that the article had attracted many more spectators than usual, and he would be able to hand over a considerable sum of money to the Dispensary as a result.

Wallsend West End: Colin Thompson, Eddie Howard, Ralph Moore, Colin Devine, Lawrence Debbage, Dave Birdsey, Matt Ovington, Ronnie Duffell, John Sanderson, Will Crawford and Gordon Cross.

Wallsend Boys' Club: John Britt, Stewart Graham, Jim Emmerson, Malcolm Hodgson, Cecil Hodgson, James Tymon, Ken Farthing, Alan Renwick, Wilf Carr, Tom Hodgson, Edwin Brown.

WALLSEND SLIPWAY / WALLSEND SLIPWAY RESERVES

North East Industrial Welfare League		1959
Tyneside League	Runners-up	1910-11, 1911-12
Tynemouth YOC League		1956
Northern Amateur League		1959

Ground: Slipway Sports Ground, Rosehill Old Field, 1908.
Secretary: S. Tiesdale, 1945. B. Sawyer.

Ran two teams in the 1940s and '50s and once had Billy Scott the former England International in their line-up. Another player, J.G. Scott left to join Newcastle United and played in the first team between 1910 and 1913 before being transferred to Grimsby Town.

Wallsend Slipway in the early 1900s.

Norman Gall, Wallsend Slipway, who played for Brighton & Hove Albion in the 1960s.

Players who went on to play league football:

Billy Scott – Brentford and England   J.G. Scott – Newcastle United
N. Gall – Brighton

Wallsend Slipway and Reserves, 1940s. Tynemouth YOC League Trophies – Northern Eastern Industrial Welfare League Shield. Includes Billy Scott, former England International, sitting front row, 4th from right.

WALLSEND COMMUNITY FC

Cramlington & District League   2006-07
Ground: Rising Sun.   Secretary: J. Weatherstone.

Right: Wallsend Community, 2006-07. Back row: A. Bruce, A. Bachelor, G. Larkin, M. Austin, D. Pace, K. Morrison, R. Glennie, M. Harrison, D. Turnbull. Front row: T. Coxon, C. Horsman, K. Stephenson, G. Charlton, C. Gilbert, A. Stobbs.

WESTERN YOUTH CLUB

Newcastle & Gateshead League   1960s
Ground: Western Fields.   Manager: J. Birse.

Left: Western Youth Club, 1967-68. Back row: A. Welsh, J. O'Donnell, K. Thompson, M. Davidson, J. Nicholson. Front row: D. Spitty, I. Mackay, N. Cherry, A. Skivington, J. Robinson, I. Maxwell.

Right: Western AFC, 1968-69. Back row: M. Davidson, A. Skivington, N. Cherry, R. Irving, B. Bryden, K. Thompson, J. Nicholson, D. Spitty, A. Thompson (coach). Front row: A. Welsh, J. O'Donnell, I. Mackay, S. Thompson (mascot), A. Smith, I. Maxwell.

WILLINGTON ST AIDAN'S

Tyneside League		1909-10
Northern Amateur League Division 2	Champions	1931-32
Northern Amateur League	Champions	1922-23, 1973-74
Northern Amateur League Cup	Winners	1948-49, 1975-76
South East Northumberland League	Champions	1969-70
South East Northumberland League Cup	Winners	1969-70
Wallsend Charity Cup	Winners	1947-48
Northumberland Aged Miners Cup	Winners	1976-77
South East Northumberland Charity Cup	Winners	1977-78

Ground: St Aidan's School, Rosehill Old Field, 1908.
Managers: M. McAndrew, J. Close, G. Willis.
Secretary: F.A. McKenna, 1930s.

One of Wallsend's oldest clubs, St Aidan's briefly changed their name to Dixon Sports for sponsorship reasons in the 1970s then reverted back after a couple of seasons before folding in the late 1980s. The club still holds its reunions every year which are always well attended.

Left: Willington St Aidan's, 1948 – Northern Amateur League Challenge Cup Winners. Also winners of Wallsend Hospital Cup. Back row: Bob Peake, Joe Wilson, Bill Muers, John McConnell, Jack Donnelly, Bill Nesbitt. Front row: Jimmy Summerley, Jim Toman, Tommy Shannon, Jack Nesbitt, Bob Burns.

Right: Willington St Aidan's Reserves, 1948. Back row: Alfie Briggs, Harry Trueman, Mick Kennedy, Vin Bell, Bill Hobman, John Ronan, John Faherty. Front row: Ralph Wilson, John Ewins, Mick Connolly, Pil Long, Bill McFadden.

Left: Willington St Aidan's, 1978. Back row: F. Carlson, T. Davison, I. Gordon, Keith, K. Rodgers, B. Mills, J. Flynn. Front row: R. Wilcox, D. Johnstone, M. Bartle, J. Close, B. Bolton, E. Elliott, B. Armstrong.

Right: St Aidan's / Dixon Sports, 1975. From back to front: R. Wilcox, B. Rowell, D. Bruce, R. McCulloch, B. Bolton, J. Conway, D. Johnstone. J. Close, D. Boyle, P. Smith, B. Cavanah, L. Wynn, I. McKinnen, B. Armstrong, B. Atherton, J. Thompson.

Left: St Aidan's 1980-81. Back row: J. Close, L. Grundy, D. Knight, J. Terryell, D. Johnstone, G. McCabe, J. Robinson, J. Lowes, J. Flynn. Front row: E. Elliott, K. Hutton, W. Charlton, P. Cain, B. Bolton, R. McCulloch, B. Armstrong, J. Lumley, L. Wynn, C. Ward.

CARVILLE BOYS' BRIGADE OLD BOYS

Newcastle City Amateur League

Ground: Rising Sun Second Ground, where Sunholme Drive is now situated.

Formed in 1956 from boys that had all attended the Carville School, they lasted a few seasons before folding in 1960.

Right: Carville Boys' Brigade Old Boys, 1959. Back row: A. Fox, R. Hill, H. Naisbett, B. Sherman, L. Debbage, T. Telford. Front row: A. Cawthorne, B. Lisle, B. Todd, B. Roper, F. Rowan.

LINDISFARNE SC

Northern Combination Challenge Cup	Winners	1980-81
Northumberland Senior Challenge Bowl	Runner-up	1978, 1979
Wallsend Charity Cup	Winners	1970-71, 1973-74
Tyneside Amateur League	Champions	2000, 2013-14
Tyneside Amateur League Cup	Winners	2000 Runners-up: 2013-14
Wallsend Summer Cup	Winners	2012
Northumberland Minor Cup	Runners-up	1973-74
North East Catholic Clubs Cup	Winners	1980-81

Grounds: Lindisfarne, Rising Sun.

Managers: B. Canfield, Alan Fletcher, F. Davidson, J. Tunmore.
Colours: White, green shorts.

Formed in 1970, the Lindisfarne had a very good Northern Combination side into the 1980s with some very good players like Chunky O'Donnell, Keith Miller and Billy Sloan turning out. The Lindy still have a team doing well and in the 2014-15 season play in the Northern Alliance Division Two.

Above: Lindisfarne Charity Cup headline, 1973-74.

Left: Lindisfarne, 1970-71. Back row: S. Fisher, E. Chandlish, A. Fletcher, P. Baker, W. Patrick, W. Bowkett, E. Skinner, R. Mooney, T. Wylie. Front row: R. Elliott, R. Wood, T. Nash, M. Cuggy, P. Stephenson.

Newspaper Report – Wallsend Charity Cup Final, 1970-71

Wallsend Celtic 1 Lindisfarne 2

Lindisfarne won the final of the Wallsend Charity Cup beating local rivals Wallsend Celtic 2-1 at Lindisfarne on Sunday. Both teams opened well and Celtic just had the edge in the first half with some good attacking football and control in midfield. It was Lindisfarne who took the lead however through Mooney, who took a cross-field ball from Montgomery and scored. Celtic came back and equalised through Scott. The second half saw a dramatic change as both teams tired and the game became scrappy. A free kick on the right punched away by Phillipson but it went straight to Wood who slammed the ball home for Lindisfarne's winner.

Northern Combination League, final table, 1981-82

	P	W	D	L	F	A	Pts
Westerhope Ex	30	26	2	2	102	18	54
Gateshead Tyne	30	22	4	4	80	28	48
Lindisfarne	30	20	6	4	93	41	46
Prudhoe	30	17	6	7	79	40	40
Swalwell	30	14	8	8	66	35	36
Whickham Sports	30	12	10	8	49	37	34
Gosforth St Nicholas	30	12	7	11	62	61	31
Crawcrook	30	11	7	12	66	56	29
Parsons Ath	30	12	5	13	74	65	29
Rose Villa	30	10	9	11	61	79	29
Winlaton Halgarth	30	12	4	14	47	61	28
Newcastle University	30	9	6	15	45	50	24
Ryton	30	5	8	17	41	75	18
Northumbria Police	30	3	8	19	42	72	14
Rising Sun	30	3	4	23	34	103	10
Burnopfield Lintz	30	1	8	21	34	106	10

Newspaper Report – Northern Combination Challenge Cup Final, 1980-81

Lindisfarne 2 Whickham Sports 1

Lindisfarne are the new holders of the Combination Cup in a keenly contested final at St James' Park. The Wallsend club side beat Whickham Sports 2-1, Kevin Cowans grabbing the winning goal just ten minutes from time. Lindisfarne wearing brand new strips donated by Vaux Breweries, had bounced back from early pressure and a 30th minute goal to take the game to their Combination League rivals. After last week's game in a noisy dressing room manager Fred Davison was lost for words. 'I can't describe how I feel.' He said 'This is my first year in charge and to win this cup is just fantastic'. But for a long spell in the first half it looked as though Fred's dream was slipping away. After a bright opening 'the Farne' were subjected to intense pressure and Mazzucchi, in goal, had some anxious moments. The Lindisfarne keeper came to the rescue in the 25th minute when he raced from his line to charge down a shot from Wright who had broken clear. But five minutes later he was left with no chance as King burst through on the left and drilled a shot into the bottom corner to put Whickham in front. LIndisfarne however, responded magnificently and leveled immediately with the Whickham defence appealing for offside Brannigan found himself in the clear, 30 yards from goal. As goalkeeper Storey charged off his line 'the Farne' number nine kept his head to hit a beautiful lob into the net. From then on Lindisfarne found their rhythm and, as the second half began, only a tremendous save by Storey kept Whickham level. Steve Turner found himself with the goal at his mercy and blasted his shot goalwards. It looked a goal all the way till Storey somehow got his body in the way and the ball flew to safety. The game was now being played in a blizzard but with the snow at their backs, Lindisfarne took advantage. The winner came when Alan Dodds squeezed a ball through for skipper Keith Miller. He took it to the bye line before squaring for Kevin Cowan's who did the rest.

Lindisfarne, 2012-13. Back row: L. Graham, P. Richardson, M. Robson, D. Moore, J. Morton, J. Briggs, P. Lowery, J. Storey, H. Singh, A. Fawcett. Front row: A. Toothill, R. Fenwick, B. Paolozzi, R. Fleming, M. Wilkinson, K. Cash, P. Strauthers.

Right: Lindisfarne FC, 2000. Back row: J. Tunmore, A. Fletcher (inset), Westgate, Ging, Hart, Mullarkey, Fleming, Savage, A Reid (inset), T. Mullarkey, ?, ?. Front row: P. Cairns, Crow, Arnott, Robinson, McIlveen, Scarth, May. G. Savage (mascot).

ORWIN NEW WINNING / ORWIN ROSEHILL

South East Northumberland League	Champions	1989-90
South East Northumberland League Cup	Winners	1989-90
Northern Alliance Combination Cup	Winners	1994-95
Northumberland Minor Cup	Winners	1993-94

Grounds: NEERC Kings Road, Lightfoot Stadium.
Secretary: S.J. Patison.   Manager: N. Bains.

WIGHAM WANDERERS

League: unknown.   Secretary: E. Cowen.
Ground: Swans Rec.   Appeared in the FA Handbook for 1956.

WALLSEND WANDERERS

Newcastle Central League 1970s   Ground: St Peter's Road.

PARSONS MARINE

North East Industrial League 1957   John Neill Trophy Winners 1958-59
Secretary: J. Baxter.   Ground: Swans Recreation.

Parsons Marine, 1959. Back row: Mr Montgomery (manager), I. Livingston, G. Allen, P. Yates, T. Harrison, D. Bartram, H. Robson, W. Hails, Mr Richards (trainer). Front row: G. Woolford, A. Scurr, L. Oman, K. Poulter, R. Wigham.

WALLSEND ENGINEERS

Northern Amateur League   1930s
Ground: Adelaide Cricket Ground, Holy Cross
Colours: Black and white quarters.   Secretary: T.W. Smith.

BRITISH ELECTRIC REPAIRS

League: unknown   Secretary: A Flannery.
Played for one season 1959-60.

NELSON VILLA

Northern Amateur League 1930s   Ground: Holy Cross.
Colours: Red and white stripes.   Secretary: J.L. Marshall.

Nelson Villa started out life as a Wallsend based team before moving to establish themselves in North Shields.

HOWDON GASWORKS FC

League: North Shields YMCA 1957   Secretary: W. Mitchelhill.
Played for two seasons in the 1950s.

NEPTUNE MARINE

Tyneside Amateur League 1954   Secretary: R. Wallace, 1945.

Tyneside Amateur League, 1953-54

	P	W	L	D	F	A	Pts
Reyrolles A	24	18	4	2	76	34	40
Montague Wel	24	14	6	4	61	30	34
Dinnington V	24	17	0	7	67	43	34
N/c Dockers	24	11	4	9	75	58	26
Rutherford TC	24	12	2	10	76	67	26
Heddon Inst	24	11	2	11	65	60	24
Lemington GW	24	11	2	11	68	63	24
Neptune Mar	24	9	4	11	70	65	22
Denton YC	24	8	5	11	63	64	21
Sigm'd Pumps	24	9	2	13	50	79	20
Coll of Com	24	8	16	0	47	91	16
Simonside M	24	6	3	15	50	78	15
Vickers Arms'g	24	4	2	18	46	82	10

KICKS LEISURE

Tyneside Amateur League 2000

NEPTUNE ATHLETIC

Wallsend & District League 1962-63

WALLSEND YC

Wallsend & District League 1962-63   Ground: Western Field.

The Youth Club was based at the Poles Huts on West Street and the team competed for a couple of seasons before folding.

ROYAL ENGINEERS

Wallsend & District League 1962-63   Ground: St Peter's Road.

Based at the Territorial Army Centre Wallsend, lasted two seasons before folding.

ANGUS UNITED

South East Northumberland League Cup   Winners   1963, 1965, 1966
                                         Runners-up 1964, 1967

Northern Combination 1967

Ground: George Angus Sports Ground.
Manager/Secretary: K. Rathmell.

A very good team in the 1960s with a side made up of the employees of the George Angus Factory. They had a fabulous sports ground with first class pitches which is now the Blue Flame Sports Ground.

Right: Angus United, 1965-66. Back row: B. Anderson, J. Watson, J. Gwynn, E. Fraser, J. Amis, J. Masters, Front row: C. Richardson, W. Whitley, M. Mullen, G. Atkinson, I. Atkinson, G. Yeoman.

NORTH EASTERN MARINE / MARINE PARK

Northern Alliance	Champions	1972-73, 1973-74
Northern Alliance Cup	Winners	1972-73, 1973-74, 1974-75, 1976-77
Newcastle City Amateur League		
South East Northumberland League		1960s
Northumberland Minor Cup	Winners	1966-67
South East Northumberland Hospitals Cup	Winners	1975-76
Newcastle Dispensary Cup	Winners	1975-76
Wallsend Charity Cup	Winners	1975-76

Ground: Marine Park. Secretaries: D. Reid, 1945. D. Rowan, 1965.

North Eastern Marine always ran strong teams in the 1950s and 60s lifting the Northumberland Minor Cup in 1967 but they really came to the fore in the early '70s with a name change to Marine Park and under the management of Tony Cassidy and Bob Lodge they had a very successful spell in the Northern Alliance. It all changed very quickly however when the management team left to join South Shields taking most of the squad with them. The club never quite recovered and folded in the 1980s.

Above: North Eastern Marine, 1957. Back row: R. Paterson, F. Paterson, Charlton, McFoe, Watson, Lovell. Front row: Dudding, Scott, Summers, Parker, Blagburn.

Left: North Eastern Marine, 1959. Back row: E. Smith, J. Birdsey, D. O'Fee, P. Smith, W. Charlton, R. Jarvis. Front row: A. Linsay, D. Cosgrove, T. Fallowfield, W. Dodds, K. Oliver.

Right: Marine Park, 1965. Back row: J. Atkinson, J. Metcalf, B. Nelson, C. Fontland, A. Smith, V. Christy. Front row: T. Henry, G. Innes, G. Irving, J. Thewlis, D. Surrey.

Right: Marine Park, 1972-73 – Northern Alliance Cup, Northern Alliance KO Cup. Back row: C. Fontland, T. Cassidy, D. Baiston, R. Macklin, G. Stoneman, W. Allen, B. Lister, R. Percy, A. Smith, T. Featherstone (trainer). Front row: A. Young, M. Marry, R. Lodge, G. Ogle, A. Adams, W. Colwill.

Marine Park, 1972. Back row: T. Young, A. Gill, J. Storey, B. Allen, D. Parkin, J. Hamilton, Front row: K. Poulter, D. Stokoe, A. Adams, B. Stabler, A. Gallon.

Northumberland Senior Cup, 1st round replay, 1970-71. Wallsend player, W. Carr (No 6), just gets above Marine Park defender, Stabler, to head past the keeper in Wallsend's 4-3 Senior Cup victory.

Left: Marine Park management committee, 1975-76 – South East Hospital Cup, Northern Alliance Challenge Cup, Newcastle Dispensary Cup, Wallsend Charity Cup. Back: R. Fallowfield, G. Heal, B. Gledson, Front: J. Anderson, T. Elliott, J. Heslop.

Northern Alliance Medal, 1972-73.

WALLSEND SCHOOLS FOOTBALL

Before 1910 any local school wanting to play competitive football had to play in the Tynemouth Schools League. That is why Henry Chambers who attended the Stephenson School, Wallsend's first schoolboy to be capped by England is down as representing Tynemouth.

The Wallsend's Schools League first started in the 1910-11 season at under 15 level with just three schools competing, Bewick, Buddle and Richardson Dees. Now although only played at under 11, the older groups 12-16 play in the North Tyneside Schools Leagues, schools football is still going strong in the town with ten teams currently competing in the league.

Battle Hill Primary became the nineteenth different name on the old trophy when they won league for the first time in the 2011-12 season after almost forty years of trying.

The magnificent League Shield, was presented by the then Mayor of Wallsend, Councillor Geo. M. Fitzsimmons in 1922; unfortunately the early winners names have been removed (1922-49) but the winners since then are:

Year	Winner	Year	Winner
1949-50	St Aidan's	1881-82	High Farm
1950-51	Western	1982-83	St Aidan's
1951-52	St Columba's	1983-4	High Farm
1953-54	Carville	1986-87	Holy Cross
1954-55	Buddle	1987-88	Hadrian Park
1955-56	St Aidan's	1988-89	High Farm
1956-57	St Aidan's	1990-91	Holy Cross
1957-58	Central	1991-92	Western
1958-59	Bewick	1992-93	High Farm
1959-60	Carville – Bewick	1993-94	Hadrian Park
1960-61	Buddle	1994-95	Holy Cross
1961-62	St Peter's	1995-96	High Farm
1962-63	Buddle	1996-97	Western
1963-64	St Aidan's	1997-98	Western
1964-65	Willington	1998-99	High Farm
1965-66	Willington	1999-2000	High Farm
1966-67	Richardson Dees	2000-01	Western – St Bernadettes
1968-69	Buddle	2001-02	Denbigh – Stephenson
1969-70	Richardson Dees	2002-03	St Bernadette's
1970-71	St Aidan's	2003-04	St Bernadette's – Denbigh
1971-72	St Aidan's	2004-05	St Bernadette's
1972-73	Buddle	2005-06	St Bernadette's
1973-74	Western	2006-07	Redesdale
1974-75	St Aidan's	2007-08	Redesdale
1975-76	St Aidan's	2008-09	St Bernadette's
1976-77	St Aidan's	2009-10	Redesdale
1977-78	High Farm	2010-11	Holycross
1978-79	St Aidan's	2011-12	Battle Hill
1979-80	High Farm	2012-13	Redesdale
1980-81	St Aidan's	2013-14	Redesdale

Right: Willington St Aidan's, under 11s, 1963. Back row: J. Durkin, P. Butler, T. Straker, N. Gay, B. O'Donnell, D. Johnson. Front row: D. Moor, S. O'Donnell, D. Bukowski, B. Smith, H. Watson.

Left: St Bernadette's RC, 2004-05. Back row: D. Mooney (Coach), J. Wigham, T. Richards, D. Mulligan, S. Allcock, R. Breene, A. Russell. Front row: A. Campbell, L. Turnbull, O. Cairns, N. Jones, J. Renwick, D. Watts.

Knock Out Cup

Once again the names on the plinth only go back to 1980-81.

1980-81	St Aidan's	1997-98	Western
1981-82	High Farm	1998-99	High Farm
1982-83	Central	1999-2000	Western
1983-84	High Farm	2000-01	High Farm
1984-85	Holy Cross	2001-02	St Bernadette's
1985-86	Hadrian Park	2002-03	Denbigh
1986-87	Holy Cross	2003-04	St Bernadette's
1987-88	Hadrian Park	2004-05	St Bernadette's
1988-89	Holy Cross	2005-06	St Bernadette's
1989-90	Holy Cross	2006-07	Redesdale
1990-91	Holy Cross	2007-08	Jubilee
1991-92	Hadrian Park	2008-09	Western – Stephenson
1992-93	High Farm	2009-10	Western – Redesdale
1993-94	Hadrian Park	2010-11	Holycross
1994-95	Holy Cross	2011-12	Denbigh
1995-96	High Farm	2012-13	Redesdale
1996-97	Western	2013-14	Redesdale

Wallsend Schools District Team

The Wallsend schools 'Town Team' chosen from the thirteen primary schools lifted the 2013-14 County Cup for the fourth time since 1974, a magnificent achievement against the much bigger district organisations.

Right: Wallsend and Tynemouth under 11s, 1963 – After County Cup Final won by Wallsend Schools.

Left: Wallsend Town Schools under 15s, 1961 Back row: ?, B. Wilkinson, ?, D. Bruce, Keenan, S. Hill, C. Fontland, A. Campion, P. Davison. Front row: R. Phillips, M. Oldfield, Nelson, A. Fletcher, T. Brookes.

Right: Wallsend under 15s, 1963 – County Champions. Back row: Mr Manning, C. Oliver, M. Allen, T. Gibson, F. Dotchin, T. Brooks, P. Smith, Mr Vale. Front row: R. Rycroft, B. Mooney, F. Woodhouse, Mr Carruthers, D. Bruce, W. Brown, A. Bloomfield.

Stephenson School

Left: Wallsend Stephenson School under 15s, 1911-12 – Tynemouth District League Champions. James Blakey at (back centre) with County Cap. Back row: Mr Jewels, G. Henderson, T. Russell, J. Blakey, T. Nichol, J. Abbott, Mr Moffat. Front row: O. Tinsdale, R. Herring, C. Lingham, J. Ryan, W. Reed, T. Blakey.

James William Blakey

A really tragic event happened in December 1912 when outstanding local schoolboy footballer James Blakey (*right*) lost his life in an accident on the River Tyne. James had just started his first job at Wallsend Slipway and was working as a fireman on a steam launch when the tragedy occurred. Earlier that year he had been a member of the successful Stephenson School team that had won the Tynemouth and District League, had been capped by Northumberland Schools and was being watched by a host of football league clubs.

The inquest came up with an accidental death verdict! It was said it was a very windy day and he must have blown overboard. It seems health and safety just didn't exist 100 years ago.

Right: Stephenson School under 15s, 1956-57. Back row: G. Parkin, J. Archer, B. Jordon, A. Gray, T. Cassidy, A. Smith. Front row: W. Kellor, C. Snowdon, L. Cox, J. Sample, R. Lodge.

Central School

Left: Central School under 13s, 1955-56. Back row: Sample, Cox, Gray, Parkin, Cassidy. Front row: Smith, Archer, Grundy, A. Smith, Flaherty, Gibbons, Brady.

Buddle School

Right: Buddle School under 11s, 1949. Back row: Mr Carruthers, E. Bolton, B. Sinclair, Mr Watson, B. Money, J. Gibbons, Mr Manning. Front row: Hedley, H. Gaddes, A. Bruce, ?, A. Finlay, A. Weavers, T. Wilson.

Left: Buddle School, 1960. Back row: D. McCarthy, K. Conroy, R. Elliott, D. Luke, G. Reay, ?. Front row: R. Winskill, G. Armstrong, J. Montgomery, J. Jones, ?.

Carville School

Right: Carville under 11s, 1957-58. Back row: Mr Gilmore, Nunn, B. Strutt, Guymer, Mr Morton. Middle row: K. Lamb, Hunter, Park, Porter, Wells. Front row: M. Earington, M. McAvoy, Phillips, Smith, Spark.

Left: Carville School, 1964-65. Back row: Mole, A. Carr, ?, Scott, Peat, Holly, ?, Robey, ?. Front row: G. Hough, ?, Aithinson, R. Wilson, N. McQuade.

Willington County Juniors School

Right: Willington County Junior School, 1964. Back row: M. Osbourne, S. Haslam, S. Lansom, E. Young, J. Mason, S. Blair, B. Bruce. Front row: S. Rowntree, M. Bird, D. Jaimeson, S. Daley, B. Lisgoe.

Hadrian School

Left: Hadrian School under 11s, 1966. Back row: B. Riley, J. Kermode, V. Ferguson, I. Wilson, A. Waddle. Front row: J. Mason, K. Miller, D. Jaimeson, S. Daley, M. Osbourne, R. Hudson.

St Aidan's School

Right: St Aidan's under 13s, 1965. Back row: N. Gay, B. O'Donnell, K. Woods, J. Connelly, B. McGuire, D. Bukowski, S. O'Donnell. Front row: D. Ashburner, D. Clark, D. Johnson, P. O'Donnell, M. Joyce, A. Fisher.

St Bernadette's School

Left: St Bernadette's, 2003-04. Back row: M. Bramley, R. Branch, J. Burn, R. Breen, A. Tunmore, D. Fairley, J. Marshall, D. Mooney (coach). Front row: W. Marsh, N. Jones, S. McNeil, J. Alcock, A. Russell, K. Gray, J. Renwick, O. Cairns

St Columba's School

Right: St Columba's under 15s, 1947-48 – League Champions, Cup Runners up. Back row: Carr, Lawlor, McKeon, Debbage, Wafer, Makay, Ruddick. Front row: Coleby, Flannery, Donnelly, Fallowfield, Brownlee.

Left: St Columba's under 15s, 1961. Back row: L. Walters, J. Gartland, D. Lawson, R. Nelson, S. Peart, R. Lilley, A. Campion. Front row: M. Bartle, D. Braddick, D. Souter, J. Graham, B. Mooney.

Right: St Columba's under 13s, 1961. Back row: H. Webb, M. Ferry, J. Quinn, D. Lawson, P. McMaughn, D. Malia, J. Lake. Front row: C. Oliver, M. Bartle, B. Mooney, A. Hobson, R. Scott.

Western School

Left: Western School under 13s, 1964-65. Back row: R. Lucas, J. Armstrong, J. Jones, M. Brownlee, R. Ion, R. Rowell, B. Allerdyce. Front row: D. Edlington, J. Ward, R. Young, R. Elliott, R. Winskill.

Wallsend Technical School

Right: Wallsend Tech under 15s, 1961. Back row: Robertson, G. Athey, J. Bell, R. Phillips, P. Preston, D. Wilkinson, M. Hogarth, D. Hall. Front row: A. Hill, D. Robinson, A. Curran, T. Limbrick, A. Fletcher, R. Walker.

Wallsend Grammar School

Left: Wallsend Grammar School, 1950-51 – League Champions & Cup Winners, Wallsend Schools League. Back row: Mr James, I. Cotis, T. Wright, L. Alderson, B. Bell, K. Penham. Middle row: D. Kay, J. Imray, J. Thornton, D. Wynn, D. Heathcote, W. Holmes, K. Parkin, Front row: B. Lisle, G. Kennedy, M. Clementson, F. Mills.

Wallsend Grammar under 13s, 1963. Back row: R. Fuller, K. Mitchell, P. Buckton, D. Wilson, J. Rowan, Vaughn. Front row: R. Staward, B. Walker, S. Chater, Mr Laffey, A. Smith, S. Barrett, J. Cecconi.

Right: Wallsend Grammar, 1956. Back row: E. Plane, ?, A. Corby, ?, D. Eltringham, B. Davison, A. Bruce. Front row: Mr Walton, ?, B. Oxley, Liddle, L. Stoves, B. Brown, J. Heron, A. Weavers, Mr Brown.

Wallsend Grammar under 15s, 1961. Back row includes: C. Jowsey, D. Whitfield, C. Tait, J. Brown. Front row: Mr Berry, J. Burton, R. Hall, D. Dunn, K. Hay, B. Anderson, ?.

English School's Trophy

Right: The programme for the English Schools' Trophy, 3rd round, between Newcastle Boys and Wallsend Boys. Newcastle won 2-0 in a game played at Newton Park, the home of Heaton Stannington AFC, in the 1967-68 season.

A newspaper report after the game said: 'The expected avalanche of goals never came – thanks to a tremendous performance by Steele in the face of relentless Newcastle pressure.'

Eric Steele, the Wallsend keeper, went on to play for Derby County and was later the goalkeeping coach at Manchester United.

The Newcastle team included centre forward Gordon Hodgson who went on to sign for Newcastle United before being transferred to Mansfield Town. In goal for Newcastle was Peter Ewart who also played for England Schoolboys.

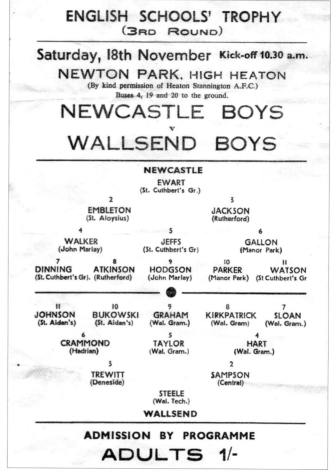

Left: The Wallsend team for the English Schools Trophy, 3rd round, against Manchester Boys at Old Trafford on Saturday 28th January 1950. Manchester won 1-0. The team was, back row: N. Hay (Western), A. Kent (Grammar), A. Beech (Grammar), B. Todd (Carville), J. Edwards (Buddle), G. Beckwith (Grammar). Front row: B. Brownlee (St Columba's), J. Swann (Buddle), B. McKay (St Columba's), A. Graham (Grammar), D. Whinn (Grammar).

Blake Cup

The premier cup of Northumberland schools football is played at under 15 level and although it has been played for over a century it has only been won a few times by Wallsend schools, notably Stephenson in the 1950s and Hadrian in the 1960s.

Right: A certificate awarded to Stanley Craig of Stephenson School for his appearance in the Blake Cup Final in 1957-58.

YOUTH FOOTBALL

There are currently three junior clubs running in Wallsend: Wallsend Boys' Club – Willington Quay and Howdon Boys' Club – Wallsend Community.

Wallsend Boys' Club

The club runs junior teams ranging from 7 to under 18s at their Bigges Main base.

Secretary: P. Kirkley.   Club colours: Green and yellow.

Wallsend Boys' Club 15s, 1989. Back row: N. Bone, P. Tait, S. Urwin, G. Monaghan, J. Winder, P. Geddes, J. Melrose. Front row: P. Mooney, T. Dinning, M. Tate, P. Bennett, T. Annom, G. Renforth, M. Riches.

Right: Wallsend Boys' Club, 1973. Back row: A. Wood, W. Rogers, J. Boulton, T. Mazzuchi, K. Lowery, T. Holmes, P. Redford. Front row: S. O'Neill, J. Rice, R. Abbott, L. Weatheril, D. Homer, ?.

Willington Quay and Howdon Boys' Club

Run teams at under 13 and under 16 and play at St Peter's Road.

Willington Quay Boys Club, 1960 – League Champions and three cups. Manager Peter Kirkley. Back row: ?, Ray Marshall, Bill Davies, Bob Pears, Len Thomas, Terry Shaw, Peter Hall. Front row: Neil Harland, John ?, George Emery, Dave Varty, Tom Davis.

Left: Mr G. Birss with Marine Park Juniors captain, Peter Smith, and Willington Quay Juniors captain, Ian Bayson, dark shirt, before League Cup Final in 1966.

Right: Willington Quay & Howdon Jnrs, 2000.

Wallsend Community

Wallsend Community run teams right through the age groups.

Ground: Rising Sun.   Secretary: J. Weatherstone.   Club colours: Dark blue.

Wallsend Community 14s, 2010-11.

Corinthians

Right: Trophies and honours won by Corinthians Jnrs, 1959-60. Back row: T. Cassidy, ?, S. Craig, B. Walker, D. Winskill, G. Mitchell. Front row: P. Durant, K. Wanless, L. Cox, C. Snowdon, N. Dunn.

St Columba's

Left: Columba's under 16s, 1946. Back row: Hagen, Wales, Higgins, Mr Reynolds. Middle row: Brecken, Campbell, Collins. Front row: Hastie, Conway, Kirby, McMullen, McDonald.

Right: St Columba's under 18s, 1952. Back row: M. Lawler, B. Carr, ?. J. Bait, T. Bianchi, R. Hillcote. Front row: T. Morrison, P. Flannery, T. Fallowfield, K. McGloughlan, B. Ruddick, J. Lavery.

Boy Scouts

Left: Wallsend Boy Scouts, 1912-13, taken at the North Road ground. You can see the Wallsend AFC on the grand stand. Winners of the Boy Scout League, 1912-1913.

SUNDAY FOOTBALL

Organised Sunday football only started after the last war, indeed the Football Association didn't give permission for it to be played until the mid 1950s and the local authorities refused to open their football grounds on the Sabbath. The Coronation Club were one of the first teams in Wallsend playing to good crowds at the Powder Monkey ground in the late 1940s and early '50s.

Sunday football really took hold with the formation of the North East Sunday League in the 1949-50 season which eventually had ten divisions and good teams like Marine Park, Buffs, Buist Garages, Engineers and the Dorset soon joined and St Peter's Road ground became very busy on a Sunday morning with some very competitive games being played in front of big crowds. It wasn't just the football but the social side of the pubs and clubs that enabled the teams to thrive, indeed the Dorset used to put a double decked bus on for their supporters to travel to away games, and it was always full!

Wallsend has produced a host of good teams over the years that have come right through the leagues only to struggle when they reached the top two divisions. The Labour Club remain the only Wallsend team to win the North East Premier League title, becoming champions three times in the 1990s and they were also Northumberland County Champions three times during the same period, a terrific achievement!

Sunday football is still very popular in the town with eleven teams still competing as against six Saturday sides.

MARINE PARK

North East Sunday League: Premier Div 1960s
Ground: Marine Park.
Folded in 1971.
Managers: J. Metcalf, B. Watson.

The North East Sunday Football League, Premier Division final placings, 1967-68

	P	W	D	L	F	A	Pts
Birds Nest	26	21	5	0	61	8	47
Dunston SC	26	17	6	3	66	27	40
St Peters Ath	26	16	5	5	74	35	37
North Heaton	26	13	7	6	65	35	33
Black Bull N/C	26	13	5	8	45	22	31
Benton SC	26	12	6	8	60	33	30
Blue Bell	26	11	6	9	69	38	28
Burnside	26	10	8	8	48	40	28
GPO	26	9	5	12	54	42	23
Runnymede	26	8	7	11	58	50	23
Terrace Inn	26	5	7	14	46	56	17
Marine Park	26	6	4	16	37	73	16
Angus United	26	3	0	23	28	166	6
Egypt Cottage	26	2	1	23	30	113	5

ENGINE INN

North East Sunday League: K Division 1971-72.
Ground: St Peter's Road.
Manager: H. Tonks.

Appeared to play for just one season before folding.

Right: Engine Inn, 1968. Back row: B. Gamble, R. Hall, C. Waddle, D. Skivington, T. Mason, A. Sample. Front row: J. Dewhirst, R. Greenwood, R. McGlen, R. McCulloch, W. McWilliam.

WALLSEND RAOB

North East Sunday League: B Division Champions 1974-75
Ground: St Peter's Road. Managers: F. Walker, J. Martin.

Sunday league stalwarts, with players like Jimmy Grieveson, Dave Milne, the terrific Jimmy McDonald and in particular Brian Breeze who turned out for the Buffs for an incredible seventeen seasons. They almost always played in the top two divisions but unfortunately folded after almost fifty years.

B Division, 1974-75	P	W	D	L	F	A	Pts
Wallsend RAOB	26	22	2	2	76	25	46
Lemington Labour	26	20	2	4	78	24	42
Westerhope CC	26	17	4	5	58	27	38
Teams SC	26	16	5	5	77	42	37
Five Bridges	26	14	5	7	47	30	33
North Heaton	26	12	5	9	41	39	29
Benton SC	26	13	1	12	51	33	27
Spenfica	26	9	7	10	48	42	25
Benton Black Bull	26	10	2	14	60	65	22
Whickham R & Crown	26	8	5	13	48	55	21
Saltwell	26	7	6	13	40	56	20
Willington RBL	26	5	2	19	32	71	12
Balloon	26	3	3	20	25	73	9
Wallsend Engrs	26	1	1	24	20	122	3

Wallsend RAOB (Buffs), 1993. Back row: Micky Blench, Paul Stokes, John Douglas, Scott Fleck, Colin Storey, Alan Taylor, Steve Cherry. Front row: Steve Pegram, Billy Cook, Steve Bailey, Iain Davison, Micky Blench Jnr, Keith Cairns.

Wallsend R.A.O.B, 1993. Back row: David Elliott, Phil Heward, Jimmy Hetherington, Paul Stokes, Colin Storey, Paul ?, Micky Blench (manager). Front row: Keith Cairns, Billy Cook, Davey Willis, Steve Bailey, Brian Young, Rob Moorhead, Geordie McEwen.

WILLINGTON QUAY RAILWAY

North East Sunday League: B Division 1971-72
Ground: Smiths Park. Manager: P. Lee.

Formed when East Howdon Social folded and the management and players started the Railway team. Won promotion to B Division in the 1970-71 season.

North East Sunday League, B Division, 1971-2							
	P	W	D	L	F	A	Pts
Coxlodge BL	26	21	4	1	76	11	46
Benton SC	26	16	5	5	69	29	37
North Heaton	26	14	4	8	43	30	32
Newcastle RAOB	26	12	8	6	50	42	32
Hillheads BS	26	13	5	8	41	32	31
Daisy Hill	26	12	5	9	55	41	29
Stargate	26	8	8	10	52	40	24
Willington Quay	26	10	4	12	48	57	24
Heaton meadowfield	26	7	9	10	48	56	23
NE Sportsmen	26	7	8	11	37	52	22
Ballon	26	9	4	13	37	61	22
Blue Vale	26	7	2	17	34	57	16
County Hotel	26	6	4	16	38	68	16
GPO	26	2	6	18	23	65	10

WALLSEND TOWN INTER

North Tyneside Sunday League 2002
Ground: St Peter's Road Secretary: J. Weatherstone.

BEWICK FC

North East Heating Trades League Ground: Flatworth.

DORSET SPORTS CLUB

North East Sunday League: E Division Champions 1968-69
C Division Champions 1976-77
Harry Oxley Cup: Winners 2002-03, 2006-07
Knock-out Cup: Winners 2006-07

Founded: 1967. Secretaries: J. Conway, H. Morgan.

Always a very well run club with the likes of Harry and Bob Brownlee, Andy Devine, Mick Cuggy and Peter Angus in their ranks. Unfortunately folded in 2009 after almost half a century.

Dorset Arms SC, 1964. Back row: B. Snell (Manager), D. Braddick, T. Davidson, J. Dewhurst, B. Brownlee, A. Devine, B. Neill. Front row: D. Elliott, A. Fletcher, H. Brownlee, M. Cuggy, D. Mooney, B. Pumfrey.

Left: Dorset SC, 1967. Back row: D. Braddick, T. Davidson, J. Powers, M. Cuggy, B. Brownley, A. Devine. Front row: D. Mooney, A. Fletcher, B. Pomfrey, D. Spark, B. Mooney.

North East Sunday League, C Division, 1976-77

	P	W	D	L	F	A	Pts
Dorset Sports	26	18	3	5	58	24	39
Lemington Comrades	26	16	4	6	48	26	36
Coxlodge & Gosforth	26	15	5	6	56	31	35
Patent Hammer	26	15	4	7	55	34	34
Forest hall RBL	26	14	5	7	46	31	33
Balloon	26	11	11	4	40	33	33
Lemington SC	26	10	7	9	66	42	27
Prudhoe WM	26	8	9	9	44	47	25
Spenfica	26	9	5	12	41	41	23
Kenton Quarry	26	9	5	12	46	62	23
Heaton Meadowfield	26	7	7	12	45	59	21
Crown & Anchor	26	6	7	13	35	41	19
Wallsend Engineers	26	3	5	18	27	75	11
Scotswood SC	26	1	3	22	20	93	5

Right: Dorset SC, 1968. Back row: A. Devine, J. Dewhurst, T. Davidson, B. Brownlee, D. Spark, P. Burns. Front row: B. Wood, P. Angus, A. Fletcher, B. Mooney, T. Nash.

EAST HOWDON

North East Sunday League: D Division 1967-68
Ground: Smiths Park.   Secretary: P. Hathaway.

D Division, 1967-68

	P	W	D	L	P	A	Pts
Robin Hood	26	23	2	1	128	20	48
Black Horse	26	19	4	3	103	39	42
Lees	26	19	2	5	100	35	40
County Hotel	26	18	3	5	99	33	39
Durham Press	26	13	6	7	90	38	32
Heaton RAOB	26	12	7	7	57	46	31
East Howdon	26	13	2	11	72	61	28
Monkseaton	26	10	3	13	61	58	23
Jesmond SH	26	9	5	12	46	77	23
Westgates	26	10	2	14	54	71	22
Rediffusion	26	4	5	17	29	86	13
N/C Supporters	26	4	2	20	39	137	10
S and Sailors	26	2	5	19	22	110	9
Honeysuckle	26	1	4	21	19	89	6

WALLSEND CARVILLE

Tyneside Sunday League: 1984

THERMAL

Ground: St Peter's Road.   Secretary: B. Anderson.

North East Sunday League, H Division, 1967-68

	P	W	D	L	F	A	Pts
Prudhoe US	26	24	1	1	101	15	49
Prudhoe WM	26	23	1	2	128	12	47
Spenfica	26	21	2	3	121	27	44
N/C & G Fire S	26	15	3	8	72	41	33
Stanley Miller	26	13	4	9	80	65	30
Seaton Cannon	26	12	5	9	56	75	29
Quarry	26	10	4	12	52	63	24
H'don Three Tuns	26	7	7	12	40	60	21
BRSA W'Gate	26	8	3	15	43	58	19
Blaydon & Dist	26	6	6	14	53	72	18
Thermal	26	5	7	14	46	79	17
Stephenson Clarke	26	5	3	18	29	82	13
Gen Accident	26	4	4	18	31	85	12
Tyne Tilers	26	2	4	20	22	145	8

WALLSEND ENGINEERS

North East Sunday League: G Division Champions 1967-68
E Division Champions 1969-70   C Division Champions 1972-73
Nick Porter Cup: Winners 1967-68
Harry Oxley Cup: Winners 1969-70, 2013-14
Knock-out Cup: Winners 1969-70
Ground: St Peter's Road.   Secretaries: F. Newton, B. Lydon, S. Gallagher.

Founded in 1966, they always had terrific sides with the likes of Ray and Alan Young in their line-up. The Engineers are still playing and are currently in C Division.

Right: Wallsend Engineers, 1969. Back row: R. Roll, M. Marshall, A. Smith, K. Elliott, G. Little, G. Atkinson, J. O'Donnell, D. Hagleburge, F. Newton, R. Roll. Front row: W. Tubman, T. Cassidy, B. Oakley, K. Duffell, J. Hamilton, G. Wilcox.

North East Sunday League, G Division, 1967-8

	P	W	D	L	F	A	Pts
Wallsend Engrs	26	25	0	1	123	23	50
Longbenton BL	26	18	1	7	67	26	37
Lemington L	26	16	5	5	69	32	37
Old Fold tavern	26	17	2	7	87	32	36
Rising Sun	26	16	2	8	72	44	34
N/C Labour	26	13	5	8	57	52	31
Travellers Rest	26	10	8	8	46	39	28
Whitehill	26	8	6	12	55	64	22
Milvain	26	9	3	14	52	65	21
Heb'n NALGO	26	8	3	15	30	70	19
Bates Welfare	26	7	4	15	45	63	18
C of Commerce	26	6	5	15	63	86	17
British Celilynd	26	6	2	18	33	68	14
Beaconsfield	26	0	0	26	21	145	0

Ray Young.

Right: Wallsend Engineers. Included are, back row: S. Craig, D. Hagleburge, J. O'Donnell, G. Little, G. Atkinson, M. Marshall, K. Elliott, G. Wilcox, F. Newton, R. Roll. Front row: B. Oakley, T. Cassidy, K. Duffell, J. Hamilton, I. Domoney.

Left: Wallsend Engineers at their Presentation Night in 1970. The photograph includes: Ray Young, A. Young, P. Davidson, D. Hagleburge, B. Bowkett, S. Craig, I. Atkinson, G. Atkinson.

WESTHOLME FARM SC

North East Sunday League: C Division 1982

Ground: Rising Sun.

Managers: B. Strutt, F. Conway, J. Robinson.

Right: Westholme Farm, 1982. Back row: B. Atherton, M. Reynolds, J. Duffy, R. Fallon, S. Clark, T. Bell. Front row: B. Fawcett, I. Brown, A. Ward, C. Smith, R. Murray, G. Muirhead, B. Wiper.

Newspaper Report – North East Sunday League, C Division, 1981-82
Westholme Farm 2 Wallsend RAOB 0

Promotion seeking Westholme Farm began well when Bobby Fawcett made a good run and his cross found Smith whose shot was blocked. The home side with Fawcett and Atherton prominent were well in command and they took the lead after 20 minutes. McPartlin, the visitors keeper, got in a mix-up with his defence and Wafer rolled the ball across the goal for Fawcett to hammer in from close range. In the second half only over eagerness prevented the home side from going further ahead.

NEW RISING SUN

North East Sunday League: F Division Champions 1998-99
                            D Division Champions 2010-11
                            C Division Champions 2011-12
Harry Oxley Cup: Winners 2010-11, 2011-12
Nick Porter Cup: Winners 2009-10
Charlie Taylor Cup: Winners 2011-12
Centenery Cup   Runners up 2013-14

Grounds: Rising Sun, Blue Flame.
Secretaries: G. Thompson, 2012. F. Davidson, F. Myers, 1960s.

Our most successful Sunday team at the moment, with good players and an ambitious management, won promotion into the Premier League in 2012-13 season.

D Division, 2010-11

	P	W	D	L	F	A	Pts
New Rising Sun	20	18	2	0	89	28	56
Fawdon Park	20	15	2	3	49	19	47
The Crockets	20	12	4	4	45	18	40
Wallsend Comrades	20	12	3	5	45	25	39
The Wheatsheaf	20	6	7	7	29	38	25
Earl Grey	20	6	4	10	28	38	19
Three Bulls Head	20	6	3	11	26	45	18
Chemfica Independent	20	5	3	12	25	55	18
Sea Horse	20	5	2	13	25	47	17
Worswick Street	20	5	1	14	20	52	16
West End	20	3	3	14	30	46	12

New Rising Sun, 2013. Names include: S. Armstrong, A. Donaghey, D. Deighton, A. Punton, L. McKenna, K. Wrightson, J. Alcock, M. Callaghan, C. Heward, M. Hope, C. Benson, P. Watson, K. Patterson, D. Elliott, J. Mann, D. Small, G. Thompson, N. Dyer, R. Sanjua, C. Bainbridge, S. Keltie, M. Ronan.

LINDISFARNE SC

North East Sunday League: J Division Champions 1969-70
Nick Porter Cup: Winners 1970-71
North East Catholic Clubs Cup: Winners 1973-74
North East Heating Trades League: Premier League Champions 1983-84

Ground: Lindisfarne.   Secretaries: D. Mooney, T. Barkus.

With good players like John Dewhurst, John Powers, Ian Atkinson, Alan Fletcher and Alan Train, the Lindisfarne were promoted right through the leagues, reaching B Division before folding in 1977. Started up again shortly afterwards and joined the North East Heating Trades League; then folded again in 1987.

Lindisfarne SC Sunday, 1972. Back row: A. Train, J. Dewhurst, E. Chalmers, T. Maxwell, B. Train, K. Lamb, B. Scraggs. Front row: W. Waddell, B. Pumfrey, H. Hodgson, D. Maxwell, B. Hutchinson.

Newspaper Report – Got It! At fourth try

Hebburn Iona 1 Lindisfarne 3, 1974-5

Lindisfarne Triumphed in an action packed cup final game against Hebburn Iona on Saturday. The game was the final in the North East Association of Catholic Clubs and Lindisfarne were making their fourth attempt to life the trophy when they met Hebburn at Reyrolles ground. Iona got off to a good start when McIntyre crashed a twenty yard shot into the roof of the net and all within the first 90 seconds of the game. Lindisfarne pressured constantly but the Iona goal kept its team constantly on the ball. The rain that fell constantly throughout the game made the ball accelerate off the turf at an amazing pace, but both sides showed good control. With only 20 minutes before the end of the game it looked as if the Farne were to be denied the goal that they had tried so hard for. But five minutes later, Moor hammered a right wing shot across the goalmouth for it to cannon off a defender into the net. LIndisfarne was now in full flight and five minutes later Sloan headed home Moor's flag kick. Iona hit back to try and save the game that had slipped from their grasp but with only less than two minutes left, Barry McDonald settled it for Lindisfarne when he forced the ball over the line past Forster.

Newspaper Report – Victory they needed
Lindisfarne SC 4 Kenton Quarry 0, 1974-5

In their final game of the season in Division D of the North East Sunday League, Lindisfarne SC needed a victory to finish either as runners-up or to sweat it out for the championship with Burradon FC. Lindisfarne attacked from the start but had nothing to show for it at half time mainly due to the Kenton keeper, Callaghan who made some fine saves. The second half however, was a different story; Bartran set the Farne on the winning trail in the 41st minute and almost immediately after, Chalmers netted after some good work by Moor. Kenton came back to force a spate of corners but they were easily dealt with and wilted again under pressure from the home attack. One of Moor's specials, a 20 yards shot that flew past Callaghan into the roof of the net in the 55th minute, put the issue beyond any doubt. Another goal from Bartram in the 60th minute made it a true reflection of the superiority the Farne had over their fourth place rivals.

Left: A friendly between Lindisfarne and a Chilian Navy XI. Captain, Doug Maxwell (yellow) and ref D. Mooney; Chilian captain and officials.

D Division, 1974-5

	P	W	D	L	F	A	Pts
Burradon SC	26	23	1	2	109	17	47
Lindisfarne	26	22	2	2	82	22	46
Wallsend RBL	26	21	2	3	85	17	44
Kenton Quarry	26	16	3	7	63	41	35
Newcastle Labour	26	11	3	12	71	70	25
Turks Head	26	11	2	13	45	50	24
Windy Nook	26	10	4	12	51	61	24
Byker Union	26	10	3	13	39	51	23
Newcastle RAOB	26	10	2	14	48	59	22
Avenue	26	8	5	13	32	54	21
Blaydon Central	26	7	4	15	38	56	18
Pelaw SC	26	6	5	15	46	76	17
Travellers Rest	26	5	4	17	29	80	14
Newcastle Chronicle	26	1	2	23	22	105	4

WALLSEND ANCHOR

North East Heating Trades League: 1981

Newspaper Report – Easy Winners
Anchor 8 Norwell 2 (Division Two)

The Anchor ran out easy winners despite going behind after 15 minutes. Malia equalised from the penalty spot and from then on it was one way traffic. Charlton, with a hat-trick, and Forster and Conroy with two goals each completed the Anchor's scoring.

ROSEHILL TAVERN

North East Sunday League:	E Division Champions 1999-2000
Gaskell Irons Cup:	Winners 2000-2001
Tyneside Sunday League	2014-15

THE BUSH

North East Sunday League:	C Division 2011-12
North East Heating Trades League:	B Division 1984
Ground: Langdale School.	Secretary: C. Whalen.

Folded at the end of the 2012-13 season.

The Bush FC, 2006-07. Back row: A. Wilmot, S. Blacklock, C. Whalen, D. Livingstone, K. Busby, P. Webb, S. Brown, S. Maddison, M. Hope, A. Punton, L. Pearce. Front row: J. Ingledew, R. McDermott, L. Coulter, J. Green, M. Hellens, G. McDermott, C. Baker.

C Division, 2010-11

	P	W	D	L	F	A	Pts
PS Lord Clyde	18	16	2	0	64	15	50
Hazelrigg Victory	18	14	3	1	56	22	45
Balloon	18	10	1	7	49	38	31
The Bush	18	7	3	8	27	36	24
Lemington Labour	18	7	4	7	33	23	22
Old Hundred	18	6	4	8	30	38	22
Wallsend Engineers	18	6	3	9	26	32	21
St Dominics	18	6	1	11	25	46	19
New Marlborough Soc	18	4	4	10	21	39	16
Red House	18	0	3	15	16	58	3

SWANS ATHLETIC

North East Sunday League: J Division 1969

Ground: St Peter's Road.   Secretaries: W. Fisher, R. Wellington, R. Clewes.

Swans climbed up to F Division but folded in 1977.

F Division, 1974-5

	P	W	D	L	F	A	Pts
Fairholm	26	24	1	1	131	18	49
Benwell Adelaide	26	23	1	2	102	15	47
Novo Castria	26	17	1	8	59	33	35
Wardley Black Bull	26	13	6	7	60	42	32
Mickley SC	26	15	2	9	74	53	32
Newland	26	12	6	7	67	50	30
South Gosforth	26	13	2	11	57	42	28
Swans Athletic	26	10	2	14	36	60	22
Blakelaw SC	26	8	4	14	39	53	20
Highfield Park Rangers	26	8	4	14	42	76	20
Wardley RBL	26	7	5	14	36	81	19
Throckley SC	26	6	4	16	33	59	16
Newcastle Adelaide	26	3	2	21	34	112	8
Wallsend RSW	26	2	2	22	20	97	6

WALLSEND CONSTITUITIONAL

North East Sunday League: K Division 1971-72

Ground: St Peter's Road.   Secretary: P. Neal.

Only lasted three seasons, promoted twice up to H Division but folded in 1974.

North East Sunday League, K Division, 1971-2

	P	W	D	L	F	A	Pts
Malting House	26	23	3	0	125	19	49
Anglo Great Lakes	26	19	4	3	69	27	42
Rankotel	26	17	3	6	64	56	37
Azure Blues	26	15	4	7	81	45	34
Queens Arms	26	14	6	6	70	47	34
Wallsend Constitutional	26	10	5	11	49	58	25
Wills Imperial	26	9	7	10	39	64	25
Newcastle Airport	26	9	5	12	51	67	23
Engine Inn	26	9	4	13	44	66	22
Flying Scotsman	26	8	3	15	50	43	19
Belgrave	26	9	1	16	53	70	19
Kimberley Clark	26	8	1	17	41	83	17
Printers	26	4	7	15	39	70	15
PO United	26	0	3	23	26	90	3

WILLINGTON ROYAL BL

North East Sunday League: B Division 1972-73

Ground: Smiths Park.   Secretary: P. Lee.
Colours: Yellow.

Formed when the Willington Railway Management moved to the Legion but only lasted two seasons before folding at the end of the 1973-74 season.

THE ANSON / MINERS

Formed 1972
North East Sunday League: K Division Champions 1972-73
                             J Division Champions 1973-74
                             H Division Champions 1974-75

Changed name to WALLSEND MINERS

North East Sunday League: G Division Champions 1975-76
                             F Division Champions 1976-77
                             E Division Champions 1977-78
                             D Division Champions 1978-79
                             C Division Champions 1979-80
Wallsend Charity Cup: Winners 1976-77

Ground: Rising Sun.   Secretaries: T. Atkinson, S. Laing, J. Grew.

Wallsend's most successful team in terms of winning league titles, eight in a row between 1972-80. The Miners were a team full of great characters like John Grew, the manager, and very good players like Tom Nolan, Paddy Cain, Terry Hannard and Decka Johnston. They started out life at the Anson Pub before moving to the Miners, then folded in the 1980s.

Right: Wallsend Miners, 1977. Back row: B. Atkins, C. Giles, D. Moaley, B. Riley, R. O'Donnell, T. Hannard, P. Smith, M. Braddick, B. Rowel. Front row: J. Grew, T. Gibson, R. Dowdle, Lee, N. Blane, D. Johnstone, J. Dowdle, K. Atkins.

North East Sunday League, H Division 1974-75

	P	W	D	L	F	A	Pts
Anson	26	22	1	3	101	22	45
Crawcrook SC	26	18	5	3	69	21	41
Campbell Park	26	15	2	9	73	39	32
Kimberly Clark	26	12	8	6	52	32	32
W.N Bay Horse	26	14	3	9	61	48	31
Gold Cup	26	12	3	11	49	41	27
Wallsend East End	26	11	5	10	53	48	27
Byker P.T.E	26	10	6	10	54	49	26
Newcastle P.T.E	26	8	5	13	45	62	21
Anglo Great Lakes	26	9	2	15	28	44	20
Maccabi	26	6	7	13	31	74	19
Scribes United	26	6	5	15	36	76	17
Killingworth SC	26	6	4	16	34	68	16
Newcastle Airport	26	2	6	18	21	80	10

Right: Wallsend Miners, 1978. Back row: J. Grew, D. Wells, D. Knight, B. Nicholson, R. Dowdell, J. Walton, T. Nolan, J. Dowdell, M. Dodds, T. Hannard, B. Stoker, B. Grant. Front row: C. Giles, P. Cain, S. King, M. Thompson, T. Gibbon, H. Wilson.

THE BARKING DOG

North East Sunday League: C Division Champions, 2003-04

Ground: Rising Sun.   Secretary: T. Banks.

Still competing, are currently in D Division.

Left: Barking Dog FC, 2011-12. Back row: R. Conder, T. Blackford, C. Ferguson, J. Gibson, J. Cox, C. Emery, D. Grieves, M. Baxter, W. Gardner, D. Routledge. Front row: D. Wheatley, M. Barnes, S. Casey, D.L. Marshall, G. Clark, T. Banks.

Right: Barking Dog FC, 2012-13. Back row: J. Smith, W. Gardner, C. Ferguson, J. Cox, M. Robertson, A. Miller, S. Casey, D. Daley, T. Blackford, C. Reynolds, D. Wheatley. Front row: J. Routledge, P. Pearson, T. Banks, G. Clark, A. Barnes, J. Gibson.

WALLSEND AQUARIANS

North East Heating Trades League: 1980

Ground: St Peter's Road.   Secretary: Mr Bartlett.

North East Heating Trades first division top Places in 1981.		
	P	Pts
Bird Inn	15	24
Aquarians	11	20
Wallsend Coronation	14	20
C & E Injections	14	19
Wallsend East End	13	20

JOLLY BOWMAN

North East Sunday League: F Division 2011-12

Ground: High Flatworth.   Secretary: P. Mavin.

Jolly Bowman FC, 2012. Back row: S. Whittle, K. McDougall, S. Blakey, P. Mavin, G. Henderson, G. McDougall, B. Keddy, S. Laidler, G. Cairns, J. Patterson, D. Vipond. Front row: N. Giles, S. Darmody, N. Clynch, D. Warrior, S. Anderson, M. Younger, I. Davison.

ROSEHILL SOCIAL CLUB

North East Sunday League: D Division 2011-12

Ground: Langdale Centre.   Secretary: P. Scott.

Right: Rosehill SC at a presentation night in 1981.

E Division, 2010-11

	P	W	D	L	F	A	Pts
Companions Club	20	14	4	2	51	17	46
Spital House	20	14	3	3	49	24	42
West Moor	20	10	5	5	42	28	35
Rosehill Social	20	9	6	5	33	30	33
Heddon St Andrews	20	9	4	7	37	34	28
Tyneview Park	20	7	5	8	35	46	26
The Windsor	20	7	4	9	39	47	25
Westerhope Excelsior	20	6	4	10	38	39	22
TW Metro	20	6	3	11	33	43	21
Corner House	20	4	3	13	29	43	15
Lemington Park	20	1	5	14	25	60	8

ROSEHILL SOCIAL CLUB MAGPIES

North East Sunday League: E Division 2011-12

Ground: Langdale Centre.   Secretary: L. Craig.

EMPORER HADRIAN

Founded 1976
North East Sunday League: H Division Champions 1980-81

Ground: St Peter's Road.   Secretary: T. Rogers.

Lasted a few short season before folding in the mid 1980s.

Newspaper Report –North East Sunday Football League Division H
Emperor Hadrian 6 Maccabi 0

This was the second meeting of the clubs in two weeks, and resulted in another win for the Hadrian. Hadrian's pressure soon paid off when Gibb picked up a loose ball on the wing and scored his first ever goal for the home side. In the one-way traffic of the half, Hadrian missed two good chances before Volpe scored number two. Volpe scored again and completed his hat-trick after Moore had picked up a poor goal kick to score the third. In the second half Hadrian pressed forward again and Brennen was unlucky to see his shot saved off the line. Volpe capped a good performance by scoring his fourth goal from Hall cross.

THE MAURETANIA

North East Sunday League: E Divison 2013

Just rejoined the North East Sunday League after a number of years.

WALLSEND EAST END SC

North East Sunday League: H Division 1974
North East Heating Trades League: Champions 1980-81, 1982-83
North East Heating Trades League Cup: Winners 1981-82

Ground: St Peter's Road.   Colours: Yellow, black shorts.
Secretaries: B. Arnold, W. McConnell. Manager: E. Elliott.

Joined the Cramlington and District League in the mid 1980s then folded after a couple of seasons.

Walsend East End Club, 1980. Back row: L. Grundy, C. White, G. Smith, R. Smith, B. Simminson, J. Terrle, J. Arkle, K. Chandler. Front row: B. Atherton, K. Gibson, K. Bennett, J. Fish, J. Bartlett, D. Johnson, J. Lumby.

North East Sunday League, J Division 1976-77

	P	W	D	L	F	A	Pts
Killingworth SC	26	22	0	4	121	18	44
Queen Victoria	26	22	0	4	135	26	44
Whin Dyke	26	20	3	3	108	28	43
Court Sports	26	16	2	8	74	46	34
Wallsend Labour	26	14	4	8	56	43	32
Thomas Wilson	26	14	3	9	101	52	32
West Wideopen	26	13	4	9	76	45	30
Emperor Hadrian	26	11	4	11	54	74	26
Fenham	26	10	5	11	63	85	25
Newburn Memorial	26	6	5	15	46	108	17
Norgas House	26	5	5	16	39	72	15
Spicers	26	3	6	17	35	95	12
Earl Grey	26	1	6	19	24	96	8
Fountain View	26	0	4	22	18	162	4

WALLSEND LABOUR CLUB

North East Sunday League:	Premier Division Champions, 1990-91, 1991-92, 1994-95
	B Division Champions 1989-90
North East Sunday League, Bob Younger Cup:	Winners 1993-94
North East Sunday League, Centenary Cup:	Winners 1991-92, 1992-93, 1994-95
Tyneside Sunday League:	Champions 2011-12

Grounds: St Peter's Road, NEEB Sports, Churchill College.
Secretaries: K. Ormond, J. Farrage.

Wallsend's most successful Sunday team ever! With a lot of quality players in the 1990s, the Labour Club are now members of the Newcastle Central Sunday League.

Wallsend Labour Club, 1992. Back row: I. Scott, A. Black, R. Wedderburn, G. McDonald, T. Mazzuchi, T. Errington, J. Hall, D. Broderick, S. Close, R. Lodge. Front row: A. Stevens, D. McDonald, T. Garwood, T. Nightingale, T. Padderson, E. Dalziel, K. Cramman, S. Ross, T. Brock.

ROSE INN

North East Heating Trades League: 1984
Tyneside Sunday League Division 2: Subsidiary Cup Winners 2011-12

Ground: High Flatworth. Secretary: A. Simpson.

BATTLE HILL SC

North East Sunday League: B Division 1976-77

Ground: St Peter's Road. Colours: Blue and white hoops.
Secretary: F. Davison.

B Division, 1976-77	P	W	D	L	F	A	Pts
North Heaton	26	20	5	1	56	20	45
Westerhope Excelsior	26	15	7	4	58	27	37
Elmfield SC	26	16	4	6	42	24	36
Saltwell	26	16	3	7	45	20	35
Battle Hill	26	13	6	7	39	26	32
Runnymede	26	13	5	8	38	41	31
Burradon SC	26	11	4	11	50	42	26
Daisy Hill	26	9	5	12	38	46	23
Byker & St Peters	26	7	5	14	43	55	19
Bleach Green	26	7	5	14	29	42	29
Whickham Rise & Crown	26	6	6	14	26	49	18
Lindisfarne	26	4	7	15	36	50	15
Jarrow Labour	26	6	2	18	21	39	14
Benton Black Bull	26	4	6	16	30	65	14

BUIST GARAGES

North East Sunday League: D Division Champions 1961-62
Harry Oxley Cup: Winners 1962-63

Ground: St Peter's Road.

A very good side that attracted a lot of support, but only lasted a few seasons before they folded.

MINERS SPORTS BAR

North East Sunday League: F Division 2013 Runners up

Ground: St Peter's. Secretary: J. Wyres.

Wallsend Miners Sports Bar, 2014. Back row: C. Pike, T. Crow, A. Crow, K. Austin, K. Bloxham, A. Dodgeson, D. Haggerston, P. Patton. Front row: B. McLaughlin, W. Pike, K. Burton, K. Robinson, R. Errington, J. Wyres, A. Skipsey.

RISING SUN WELFARE

North East Sunday League: J Division 1968

Ground: Rising Sun. Secretaries: J. Hooks, G. Tubman, T. Lormor.

G Division, 1972-73	P	W	D	L	F	A	Pts
Lemington Comrades	26	26	0	0	106	13	52
Peacock United	26	18	5	3	64	31	41
Highfield Park R	26	15	3	8	81	49	33
Roy's SC	26	12	3	11	71	57	27
St Dominic's	26	11	4	11	70	48	26
Wallsend RSW	26	8	10	8	41	48	26
Throckley Union Jack	26	9	7	10	60	53	25
Swans	26	10	5	11	42	39	25
Jesmond Punchbowl	26	9	7	10	44	50	25
Throckley SC	26	9	7	10	41	47	25
Corvette	26	10	4	12	63	60	24
Newland	26	5	7	14	38	71	17
Maccabi	26	4	2	20	30	100	10
Three Mile	26	3	2	21	23	108	8

WALLSEND RB LEGION

North East Sunday League: D Division 1974

Ground: St Peter's Road. Secretarys: F. Davison.

Appeared in the handbook for a couple of seasons in the mid 1970s.

SHIP INN

North East Sunday League: Sportsmanship Cup Winners 2009-10

Appeared briefly in the league, before folding.

CORONATION SC

North East Sunday League:	D Division Champions 2001-02
Nick Porter Cup:	Winners 1998-99
Gaskel Irons Cup:	Winners 1998-99
Harry Oxley Cup:	Winners 2007-08
Charlie Taylor Cup:	Winners 2007-08

Grounds: Powder Monkey, Rising Sun.

One of our oldest Sunday football clubs, had a resurgence in recent years before folding again.

Wallsend Coronation Club, 2008. Back row: ?, ?, D. Martin, ?, M. Sizer, J. Patterson, J. Roys, G. Carrick, D. Hope, P. Doherty, G. Roughead, ?, A. Reid. Front row: P. Taylor, Lamb, C. Laws, T. Geddes, L. Sword, C. Phillips.

HIGH HOWDON SC

North East Sunday League: D Division 2013-14

Ground: High Flatworth.

NEPTUNE ATHLETIC

Whitley Bay Sunday League: 1965-66

WALLSEND COMRADES

Founded 1976
North East Sunday League: H Division Champions 1978-9
                                      E Division Champions 1999-2000

Ground: Rising Sun.   Secretaries: G. Heal, N. Blain, S. Dodds.

The Comrades is one of Wallsend's longest serving clubs. They are currently operating in B Division under the name of 'Rising Sun Comrades'.

Wallsend Comrades, 1990. Back row: ?, T. Sword, D. Radwell, D. Knight, R. Newton, J. Dobson, V. Symons, H. Willis, S. Turner. Front row: M. Thompson, I. Champney, M. Wilson, D. Swaddle, R. Muirhead, T. Armstrong

North East Sunday League, K Division 1976-7

	P	W	D	L	F	A	Pts
Jubilee	26	26	0	0	149	7	52
Wallsend Comrades	26	22	2	2	139	11	46
East End Catholic	26	21	2	3	107	31	44
Tyne Gas	26	16	2	8	95	37	34
Green Tree	26	14	3	9	78	44	31
Station	26	15	1	10	70	62	31
Hydraulic	26	14	0	12	63	55	28
Fox & Hounds	26	11	2	13	59	65	24
Transtar	26	8	5	13	36	66	21
Sunday Sun	26	4	5	17	24	102	13
Hibernian	26	3	6	17	26	83	12
Admin	26	5	2	19	26	113	12
CAD (NE)	26	3	4	19	22	100	10
Buma	26	2	3	21	23	132	7

WALLSEND TOWN

North East Sunday League: 2014-15

Ground: Langdale School.   Secretary: D. Grandini.
Colours: Blue and black stripes.

OVER 40s

Wallsend Town Inter, over 40s. Back row: S. Parkin, J. Smith, T. Jones, R. Brown. Middle row: J. Weatherstone, M. Yeoman, P. Charlton, A. Doyle, M. Cockburn, D. Hall, I. Foster, B. McClaren, G. Vertyn, A. Costello. Front row: J. Dabbs, M. Carr, M. Douglas, R. Lyons, G. Brooks, D. Galston, D. Mitchell, C. Strophair.

Wallsend The Bewick over 40s. Back row: K. Mills, K. Redfearn, L. Wynn, R. McCulloch, E. Beasley, M. Wilson, J. Lamn, J. Wilson. Front row: J. Miller, A. Fletcher, G. Saunders, G. Saunders (Mascot), K. Hutton, D. Johnstone, J. Sample.

Wallsend BC Winstonians Over 40s, July 2014. Back row: A. Roy (manager), C. Shilton, A. Perry, D. Nylander, S. Clarke, R. Machin, A. Hughes. Front row: M. Wells, P. Carr, J. Wesencraft, I. Cusack, J. Robertson, R. Cairns.

D Knight's over 40s Batchelor Party around 2000. Back row: M. Joyce, R. McCulloch, R. Young, D. Knight, ?, E. Anderson, ?, ?, P. Caine. Front row: J. Gouley, A. Temple, R. Palmer, R. Muirhead, J.A. Devine, J. Close, M. Thompson, ?, T. Paddison.

LADIES FOOTBALL

Ladies football is getting more popular throughout the country and although Wallsend Ladies were a very successful team in the 1970s and '80s and indeed produced one England International in Christine Hutchinson there are currently no ladies teams competing in the town.

Ladies football is nothing new however as Swans, Hood Haggies and the Slipway ran teams to raise money for the war effort during the First World War.

WALLSEND LADIES

Hull and District League	Champions 1976-77
Hull and District League	League Cup Winners 1976-77
North Eastern League	Champions 1977-78, 1978-79
North Eastern League	League Cup Winners 1978-79, 1979-80

Formed: 1971. Ground: Wallsend Sports Centre.

Manager: V. Eland.

Ran till 1980 then changed their name to Percy Main when offered the use of their ground rent free.

Left: Wallsend Ladies, 1979. Back row: D. Riseborough, S. Mears, K. Balion, ?, D. Smith. Front row: K. McShane, J. Dodds, W. McGibbon, C. Hutchinson, Fiona ?, J. Revel.

Right: Wallsend Boys Club, Girls under 14s, 2007. Back row: Danielle ?, Bethany Melling, ?, Mr Jason Melling, Rachel Kindley, Sophie ?, Rebecca Napier, Lauren McGovern. Front row: Gabi Ord, Chelsea Cairns, Hayley Pattinson, Katherine Grainger, Samantha Day, Abby ?, Katherine Bremner.

CHARITY FOOTBALL GAMES

Charity games were played right up till the 1980s and raised a lot of money for good causes. The Wallsend Charity Cup was the big competition in the Wallsend area, started as a replacement for the Wallsend Charity Shield. The games were always keenly fought out between the local rivals and attracted big crowds, the only record I can find of the winners are:

Year	Winner	Year	Winner
1945	Cramlington Welfare	1961	Rising Sun
1946	Rising Sun	1962	Corinthians
1947	Naval Yard	1963	St Columba's
1948	St Aidan's	1964	Wallsend Athletic
1949	Rising Sun	1965	Wallsend Athletic
1950	St Luke's	1966	Wallsend AFC
1951	Rising Sun	1967	Wallsend AFC
1953	Corinthians	1970	Corinthians
1954	St Luke's	1971	Lindisfarne SC
1955	St Luke's	1972	Wallsend Celtic
1956	Heaton Stannington	1974	Lindisfarne SC
1957	Rising Sun	1975	Wallsend Miners
1958	Corinthians	1976	St Aidan's
1959	Corinthians	1981	St Aidan's
1960	Naval Yard		

Above: Jack Miller, winner of five Wallsend Charity Cups with St Luke's, Rising Sun (3) and Cramlington Welfare.

Right: Wallsend Athletic captain, Eddie Mann, receives the Wallsend Charity Cup from Albert Stubbins after their 3-0 victory over Naval Yard in 1964.

The Mayor of Wallsend, Councillor Chute, presents winners Heaton Stannington with the Wallsend Charity Cup at the presentation at the Coronation Club in 1956, after their 2-0 victory over Corinthians.

Right: Wallsend Charity Cup Final – Walker Naval Yard (dark strips) v Wallsend Athletic – 1960. Won by Naval Yard.

Left: Wallsend St Columba's, 1961 – Wallsend Charity Cup. Back row: T. Morrison, M. Burly, D. Robson, P. McGloughan, J. Brass, A. Innes, Mr McGloughlan. Front row: Dixion, J. Summers, P. Doran, R. Rooney, A. Thompson, B. Jaimeson.

Right: Wallsend Corinthians, 1963 – South East Northumberland League Cup, Wallsend Charity Cup, South East Northumberland KO Cup. Back row: S. Beutiman, D. Johnstone, B. Higgins, N. Laverick, R. Nichol, ?, ?, T. Case. Middle row: ?, A. Wiseman, T. Flannery, B. Deagle, J. Flannery. Front row: P. Flannery, B. Walker, S. Jackson, J. McDonald, K. Flannery, R. Jarvis.

MATCH REPORT FROM LOCAL NEWSPAPER, 1955

WALLSEND CHARITY CUP FINAL
ST LUKE'S 3   RISING SUN 2

A big crowd attended the final played at North Road ground and watched St Luke's race into a 3-0 first half lead with goals from Hiftle, Miller and Stephenson. There looked to be no way back for the Sun, but an early goal just after half time by Howe and then another by Knox midway through the half had the Saints hanging on. Although the Rising Sun laid siege to their opponents goal in the final minutes, St Luke's defence stood firm and they hung on for a famous 3-2 victory.

The Wallsend Charity Cup Final, 1955 – St Luke's v Rising Sun. Robson the St Luke's centre half plays the ball back to keeper Tubman, challenged by Howe and Brownlee.

ST LUKE'S
TUBMAN, L. CHARLTON, REDHEAD, E. CHARLTON, ROBSON, FAIRLEY, ALLAN, MILLER, DOBSON, HIFTLE, STEPHENSON.

RISING SUN
YOUNG, W. RICHARDSON, SWAN, DUDDING, MCKAY, WILL DODDS, WAL DODDS, HOWE, BROWNLEE, HERON, KNOX.

Right: Wallsend Celtic, 1970, with South East Hospitals Cup. Back row: J. Powers, C. Oliver, B. Strutt, A. Park, P. Baker, J. Hackworth, B. Wood, J. Mann, T. Strutt. Front row: R. Elliott, M. Bartle, J. Powers, R. McCulloch, M. Cuggy, D. Elliott.

On Good Friday 1910 a charity game was played at the North Road ground, the home of Park Villa, between the Wallsend Licenced Victualers and Wallsend Miners. The line ups were:

VICTUALERS XI

HUNTER (Queen's Head), WHITE (Jolly Sailors), ROBINSON (Coach & Horses), REYNOLDS (Station Hotel), ROBERTSON (Anchor), HEWITT (Railway), HEDLEY IRWING (Ship), IRWING (Black Bull), MCINTOSH (Commercial), SPROAT (Winning), HUDSPETH (Ship).

MINERS XI

CARTWRIGHT, FOSTER, MCGOWAN, JONES, KENT, JOHNSTON, HARRISON, HUNTER, CARTWRIGHT, ADAMS, HAYES.

I don't know who won the game or how much money was raised but I bet the after match celebrations in the pubs on the High Street went on long after the final whistle.

On 24th May 1917 there was a charity game played in Wallsend between Frank Cuggy's XI and Bill McCracken's XI which attracted a crowd of 15,000. The game was used to raise money for the war effort and was thought to be played at The Avenue, the home of Elm Villa. Frank, a local boy and captain of Sunderland, and Newcastle United stalwart, Bill McCracken, chose teams that included a significant number of Sunderland and Newcastle players. Just for the record McCracken's XI won the game 1-0.

Right: The Newcastle United team at the outbreak of the First World War including Bill McCracken. Back row: Cameron (director), Hay, Watt (secretary), McCracken, Low, McPearson (trainer), Lawrence, Finlay, Hudspeth, J.P. Oliver (director). Front row: Cooper, King, Hall, Hibbert, Wilson.

Left: Sunderland AFC with Frank Cuggy, back row, first left.

Also active raising money during the First World War were ladies football teams. With most of the young men called up for the services, women's football games attracted large crowds and Wallsend had sides from Hood Haggies, Swan Hunters and the Slipway playing regularly at various venues and raising a lot of cash.

Above: Wallsend Slipway Ladies, 6th August 1917. Played at North Road Ground, home of Wallsend FC.

Left: Swans Ladies football team, 1917.

Right: Hood Haggies Ladies football team, 1917.

THE FIRST ELEVEN

Here are the men who have made Wallsend football happen down the years. Some have called them the second eleven, I like to think of them as the 'First' because without them football just wouldn't have taken place, they organised the teams, raised the money, went to all the meetings, put the post and nets up etc etc. People like:

PERCY MIDDLEMAST – who gave a lifetime to St Luke's and established them as one of Wallend's top clubs for a couple of decades.

BILLY TODD – Wallsend Gordon, a real character about whom everyone had a favourite football story.

TOMMY MORRISON – dedicated to football, served St Columba's for over thirty years.

JOE JUSTICE and JOE POWERS – always worked as a team after running the Thermal, they moved to establish Wallsend Celtic as a force in local football.

PURVIS HATHAWAY – at the helm of Cooksons for a lot of years, lovely man!

CYRIL MARR – well known in local football circles, Cyril helped re-form Wallsend Athletic in the early 1960s and was a dedicated servant to the club for thirty or so years till it folded.

BOB (STABBER) CANFIELD – mainly known for his work with Athletic, where he spent a number of successful years with Cyril Marr, before moving to the Lindisfarne where he helped set up a very strong combination team.

JACKY TUNMORE – a real stalwart known for his work with St Columba's, Swans United and Lindisfarne SC from where he has just retired in 2011 after managing teams for 50 years.

HARRY GIBSON – a smashing fella who not only managed teams well into his seventies but was also a referee from 1924-60. Ran St Luke's Reserves and formed Park Villa when St Luke's folded in the early '60s.

JOHN GREW – a larger than life character who managed a very underrated Miners team to a lot of success.

ERNIE GUSTARD – Rising Sun, a big part of the Sun's success in the '40s and '50s.

GEORDIE GILCHRIST – Rising Sun, another one of their successful management teams.

Percy Middlemast.

Tommy Morrison.

Joe Powers.

Purvis Hathaway.

Jack Tunmore.

Ernie Gustard.

John Grew.

Harry Gibson, Park Villa manager in 1970, flanked by P. Martin and T. Strutt.

JACK TUBMAN and GEORDIE TUBMAN – two different generations who made sure the Rising Sun ran smoothly down the years, long after the colliery had closed.

BILL DEAGLE – another one of Wallsend's stalwarts who was involved with Corinthians for years before helping to set up Wallsend FC in the 1960s.

JIMMY CLOSE – a terrific lad, a very enthusiastic manager, did a great job with St Aidan's down the years. He is still involved organising their annual reunions.

JIMMY MARTIN – totally involved with the Buffs team, did a great job.

PETER KIRKLEY – probably the best known youth football manager from Wallsend down the years. Did great jobs with Willington Quay and Howdon Boys' Club, Rising Sun Jnrs and Wallsend Boys' Club in a life dedicated to junior football.

JOHN WEATHERSTONE – does a great job with Wallsend Community FC.

JOHN MANN – one of the men we love to hate, still refereeing at the age of 81.

As football fans we all owe these lads and many more too numerous to mention a massive THANK YOU!

George Gilchrist.

Jacky Tubman.

Peter Kirkley.

John Mann.

And Finally ...

And now to finish the book is my team of very good Wallsend players I've watched in my lifetime – not the lads who turned professional but those who played for the sheer enjoyment. The hard part was who to leave out, but here we go:

Willie Young
(St Luke's)

Billy Oakley   Bob McKay   Peter Baker   Billy Lisgoe
(Wallsend FC)   (Rising Sun)   (Celtic)   (Wallsend Town)

Peter Flannery   Jimmy McDonald   Tony Cassidy   Walter Dodds
(Corinthians)   (Corinthians)   (Marine Park)   (Rising Sun)

Billy Wright   Ray Young
(St Columba's)   (Wallsend FC)

Subs: John Montgomery (Wallsend Town), Alan Young (Wallsend FC),
Malcolm Peel (St Columba's), Mick Cuggy (Celtic), Bob Brownlee (Rising Sun),
Ian Domoney (Engineers)

I'm sure those of you lucky enough to have seen these lads play will agree it's a very good side. Maybe you would have included someone different, but that has always been the great attraction of football, everyone has their own opinions.

Index of Saturday teams

ANGUS UNITED 79
BIGGES MAIN FC 66
BRITISH ELECTRIC REPAIRS 78
CARVILLE BOYS' BRIGADE OLD BOYS 75
CARVILLE FC 55
CARVILLE POWER STATION FC 65
CLELANDS FC 65
COMMERCIAL PLASTICS 44
COOKSONS FC 54
HADRIAN UM 35
HIGH HOWDON SC 55
HOOD HAGGIES FC 43
HOWDON ADULT SCHOOL 37
HOWDON AMATEURS 35
HOWDON BRITISH LEGION 7, 45
HOWDON GASWORKS FC 78
HOWDON ST MARY'S 39
HOWDON ST PAUL'S 39
HOWDON STEAD MEMORIAL 42
HOWDON WANDERERS 35
KICKS LEISURE 79
LINDISFARNE SC 75
MONITOR ENGINEERING FC 51
NEERC 50
NELSON VILLA 78
NEPTUNE ATHLETIC 79
NEPTUNE MARINE 79
NORTH EASTERN MARINE / MARINE PARK 9, 80
ORWIN NEW WINNING / ORWIN ROSEHILL 77
PARMETRADA FC 55
PARSONS MARINE 78
POINT PLEASANT ROVERS 33
RISING SUN 5, 8, 11, 58, 123
ROSEHILL AMATEURS 40
ROSEHILL ATHLETIC 42
ROSEHILL HILLSIDE 42
ROSEHILL VILLA 40
ROYAL ENGINEERS 79
ROYAL OAK FC 38
ST CHRISTOPHER'S 35
SUNHOLME AMATEURS 65
SWINBURNE UNITED 67
SHELL MEX FC 44
SWANS FC 11, 42

SWANS UNITED 68
THOR TOOLS 44
VICTOR PRODUCTS FC 53
WALLSEND AMATEURS 36
WALLSEND ATHLETIC 9, 47
WALLSEND BOYS' CLUB (SENIORS) 46
WALLSEND BRITISH LEGION 45
WALLSEND CELTIC 63, 123
WALLSEND COLLIERY EXCELSIOR 34
WALLSEND COMMUNITY FC 72
WALLSEND CO-OP 65
WALLSEND COMPANIONS FC 54
WALLSEND CONGREGATION 35
WALLSEND CORINTHIANS 8, 49, 122
WALLSEND ENGINEERS 78
WALLSEND ELM VILLA 36
WALLSEND FC 51
WALLSEND GORDON 9, 12, 65
WALLSEND MINERS 60
WALLSEND OLD BOYS' FC 39
WALLSEND PARK VILLA / WALLSEND AFC 6. 31
WALLSEND PARK VILLA 60
WALLSEND SLIPWAY 3, 71
WALLSEND ST COLUMBA'S 60, 122
WALLSEND ST LUKE'S 7, 56, 123
WALLSEND ST MICHAEL'S 44
WALLSEND ST PETER'S 43
WALLSEND THERMAL FC 69
WALLSEND TOWN 52
WALLSEND TRADESMEN 53
WALLSEND WANDERERS 78
WALLSEND WEST END 69
WALLSEND YC 79
WATERFORD FC 34
WESTERN YOUTH CLUB 72
WIGHAM WANDERERS 77
WILLINGTON ATHLETIC 6, 28
WILLINGTON NORTH END 40
WILLINGTON QUAY SAINTS 55
WILLINGTON PRESBYTERIANS 40
WILLINGTON ROYAL BRITISH LEGION 67
WILLINGTON ST AIDAN'S 1, 73
WILLINGTON UM 38
WILLINGTON WEDNESDAY 40